Intelligent Guides to Wines

G000075246

Alsace

2021 Edition

Benjamin Lewin MW

Preface

The first part of this guide discusses the region of Alsace and explains the character and range of the wines. The second part profiles the producers. There are detailed profiles of the leading producers, showing how each winemaker interprets the local character, and mini-profiles of other important estates.

In the first part, I address the nature of the wines made today and ask how this has changed, how it's driven by tradition or competition, and how styles may evolve in the future. I show how the wines are related to the terroir and to the types of grape varieties that are grown, and I explain the classification system. For each region, I suggest reference wines that illustrate the character and variety of the area.

In the second part, there's no single definition for what constitutes a top producer. Leading producers range from those who are so prominent as to represent the common public face of an appellation to those who demonstrate an unexpected potential on a tiny scale. The producers profiled in the guide represent the best of both tradition and innovation in wine in the region. In each profile, I have tried to give a sense of the producer's aims for his wines, of the personality and philosophy behind them—to meet the person who makes the wine, as it were, as much as to review the wines themselves.

Each profile shows a sample label, a picture of the winery, and details of production, followed by a description of the producer and winemaker. Each producer is rated (from one to three stars). For each producer I suggest reference wines that are a good starting point for understanding the style. Most of the producers welcome visits, although some require appointments: details are in the profiles. Profiles are organized geographically, and are preceded by maps showing the locations of producers to help plan itineraries.

The guide is based on many visits to the region over recent years. I owe an enormous debt to the many producers who cooperated in this venture by engaging in discussion and opening innumerable bottles for tasting. This guide would not have been possible without them.

Benjamin Lewin MW

Contents

Tables

Appellation Maps

Producer Maps

Overview of Alsace

Alsace must surely have the most picturesque villages and vineyards in France. Driving along the Route des Vins from Strasbourg to Colmar, you pass through an endless series of wonderfully preserved medieval villages. This is quite surprising considering that the region has changed hands several times in wars between France and Germany. Germanic influence has impacted wine production, from the types of grape varieties to the mix of dry and sweet styles. It is no accident that Alsace is the only region in France where the focus is as much on grape varieties as appellations. Its history has also had a significant effect on aspirations to quality (or lack thereof).

You are always conscious of the Vosges mountains. Vineyards extend eastward from the lower slopes of the mountains. Most of the best vineyards are on the middle slopes between 200 and 350m, which are a degree or so warmer than the land above or below. From the relatively narrow band of vineyards, the land opens out to the east on to a plain extending to the Rhine (which however is too far away to have any direct influence on the climate). The Vosges mountains are the dominant climatic influence. "Bad weather stops on the Vosges," they claim locally. Because rainfall is absorbed by the Vosges, Alsace has the driest vineyards in all France.

The cool climate has historically forced a concentration on white grape varieties. Grown since the fifteenth century, Riesling is an old variety in Alsace. Gewürztraminer and Muscat date from a century later. Pinot Gris was probably first grown in Alsace in the seventeenth century: it used to

Bad weather stops on the Vosges.

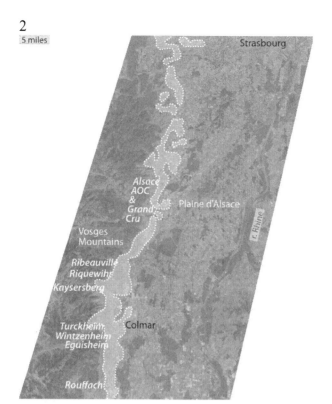

5 miles

Strasbourg

Alsace AOC & Grand Cru

Plaine d'Alsace

Vosges Mountains

r. Rhine

Ribeauvillé
Riquewihr

Kaysersberg

Turckheim
Wintzenheim
Eguisheim

Colmar

Rouffach

The vineyards in AOP Alsace form a band parallel with the Vosges mountains running from Strasbourg to south of Colmar. To the east of the vineyards, the Plaine d'Alsace extends for about 15 miles to the Rhine.

be called Tokay d'Alsace, reflecting the (improbable) legend that it was brought from Hungary, but the rules now ban use of this name because of supposed confusion with Tokaji.

Today the most important varieties are Riesling and Gewürztraminer, each with about 20% of plantings; Pinot Gris is a little lower at 15%. Fifty years ago, the most important variety was the nondescript Sylvaner, which is now disappearing from view, together with the even more characterless Chasselas. The other big difference is that the global warming trend has led Pinot Noir to increase from insignificant amounts to about 10% of plantings. Total plantings have increased from 12,000 ha in 1982 to just over 15,000 ha today.

Virtually all approved vineyards in Alsace are AOP (Appellation d'Origine Protégé). Unusually for France, the AOP is organized in terms of varietals rather than regions, and almost all wines are labeled with the name of a single grape variety. This means the wine is a monovarietal, except for Pinot Blanc. Nominally Pinot Blanc is the most commonly produced variety in Alsace, but because of a historical mix-up, wines can be called Pinot Blanc when they contain Auxerrois, a much inferior variety. Roughly two thirds of the grapevines that were classified as Pinot Blanc are really Auxerrois, so many wines labeled as Pinot Blanc actually contain a majority of Auxerrois.

The Edelzwicker and Gentil categories come from blending varieties. Edelzwicker can contain any blend of varieties; Gentil must have at least half Riesling, Pinot Gris, Gewürztraminer, and Muscat. But essentially both categories are always entry-level wines.

Besides the still wines, there is a good deal of sparkling wine, labeled under its own AOP as Crémant d'Alsace. In fact, Alsace is the second-largest producer of sparkling wine in France, after Champagne. Most often based on Pinot Blanc and Auxerrois, it is about a quarter of all production. Much of the real Pinot Blanc is used for Crémant. But Crémant is rarely a focus for quality; it may be significant that few of the producers I visited in Alsace included Crémant in what were often very long tastings.)

Alsace's reputation for quality wines is a feature of the past half century. The wines used to be regarded as low quality, mass production—what the French call vins de comptoir. One story dates this reputation from the period when Alsace came under German control following the war of 1870, and production was used to improve German wines. But in fact, Alsace had 65,000 hectares of vineyards (five times today's plantings!), mostly given over to high-yielding, low quality grape varieties, when the war started. Nor did production habits change when Alsace became French again after the First World War. Quality varieties began a slow takeover after the AOP finally came into full effect in 1962, but it was not until 1980 that the last low-grade varieties were legally excluded.

In spite of the move to quality, Alsace has been undergoing an identity crisis for years. There is a great difference between the cheap wines produced by most negociants or cooperatives and the quality wines produced by independent growers (and by some producers who have vineyards but also buy grapes). A major problem is that yields are far too high (although good producers will be well below the legal limits.) There is no agreement on style, so that wines that are not specifically identified as late harvest may range from dry to off-dry or even relatively sweet depending on the vintage. A proposal to require *Sec* on the label for dry wines has been stuck for years.

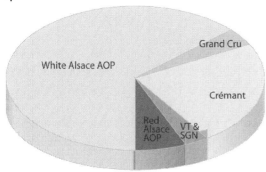

The great majority of Alsace production is white Alsace AOP. Crémant is the second major category. Red Alsace has become significant. Grand Cru and VT/SGN remain small categories.

Yields have been reduced only slowly from the bad old days, from a maximum of 120 hl/ha in 1974, to 96 hl/ha in 1982, to 80 hl/ha today. (Yields are less if a specific vineyard is named.) Yield limits are the same for all grape varieties. Applying limits to each variety (as opposed to total production in the vineyard) became the rule only in 1999 (until then, the average for any vineyard/grower had to conform to the limit, but one variety could be above and another below it). Maximum yields are much higher than elsewhere in France; only Champagne is higher. Quality would be improved by restricting yields, but "the large negociants and cooperatives are against it," explains Céline Meyer of Domaine Josmeyer. Independent growers are in a small minority.

Most wines of interest come from small family estates, making wine exclusively from their own vineyards, with the notable exception of a couple of houses, particularly Hugel and Trimbach, who function as negociants as well as growers. There is not the same market for grapes here as (for example) in Burgundy, which would allow small estates to supplement their production by buying high-quality grapes. Most growers who do not make wine sell their grapes to negociants or send them to the cooperative. In the northern extremity of the region, close to Strasbourg, the cooperative (Roi Dagobert) is dominant, and few growers produce estate wines. Elsewhere it is more of a mix.

The AOP has somewhat of an attitude of laissez-faire and does not, for example, specify the method of harvest, or the length of time wines must age before release. Machine harvesting is common on the plain, but most top growers use manual harvesting; indeed, on the steep slopes of many grand crus it would be hazardous to use machines. When a grower states that harvesting is manual, therefore, it's intended to be an indication of quality.

The Label	
Alsace AOP	Comes from anywhere in the appellation; usually a blend from several vineyards.
Alsace AOP with an individual name	The name may be either be one of 13 communes, in which case the wine may come from more than plot in the commune, or a *lieu-dit*, in which case it will come from a single vineyard.
Sec	Sec indicates that a still wine is dry, although there is some wiggle room in the regulations, so wines may not be absolutely bone dry.
Alsace Grand Cru	Comes from one of the 51 grand crus, which will be named on the label. Most grand cru wines are Pinot Gris, Gewürztraminer, or Riesling, but Muscat is sometimes found.
Grape Variety	Sylvaner, Pinot Blanc (which includes Auxerrois), Muscat, Pinot Gris, Gewürztraminer, or Riesling indicates that the wine consists of that variety. Gentil or Edelzwicker means that it is a blend of any of these varieties.
Vendange Tardive	Wine from late harvest grapes, always quite sweet, sometimes with a little botrytis.
Selection de Grains Noble	Very late harvest from botrytized grapes, always very sweet. Usually comes from Pinot Gris, Gewürztraminer, or Riesling.
Crémant d'Alsace	Sparkling wine that is described by the same categories as Champagne. Brut is dry. Demi-sec or Sec would be sweet. Can come from any of the grape varieties, but often based on Pinot Blanc.

The appellation system in Alsace is unique in France. There are only two levels of appellation for dry still wines: AOP Alsace, and AOP Alsace Grand Cru (the grand cru is named on the label). The 51 grand crus were created over a protracted period: Schlossberg was the first in 1975, then a large group followed in 1983, and another group in 1992. They cover 10% of the vineyard area, but account for only 5% of production, as yields are lower (originally 70 hl/ha but reduced to 55 hl/ha in 2001).

Terroirs vary widely. The common feature for the best vineyards is elevation: all are on the slopes of the Vosges, sometimes quite steep, often rising up sharply from a village. Grand crus are restricted to Riesling, Gewürztraminer, Pinot Gris, and Muscat (actually there is very little of the last). (Other varieties, such as Pinot Noir, can be planted, but cannot be labeled as Grand Cru.)

There are special regulations for sweet dessert wines. Wines from grapes with more than a certain sugar level can be labeled as Vendange Tardive (late harvest), and may have some botrytis. At higher sugar levels, Selection des Grains Nobles comes exclusively from botrytized grapes. Both VT and SGN are restricted to the same four varieties as the grand crus.

The Grape Varieties

The best grape varieties of Alsace are distinctly aromatic. The lesser varieties of Chasselas and Sylvaner make pleasant wines for summer quaffing but rarely have much interest. Occasionally you find an old vines cuvée, where lowered yields have brought some character; usually this takes the form of more savory, herbal impressions: interesting in their own way for showing a different potential of the variety, but not rising to the level of the noble varieties.

Pinot Blanc might make an interesting wine, but as it is usually mostly Auxerrois, it tends to lack flavor interest. In fact, I am not sure I have encountered a single Pinot Blanc in Alsace that was made exclusively from the named variety. I have found some monovarietal Auxerrois, with vieilles vignes cuvées from Josmeyer and Paul Blanck really demonstrating an unusual level of character.

Chardonnay is permitted in Alsace for the sparkling Crémant, but not for still wine. "Few people can see the difference between an Auxerrois vine and a Chardonnay; quite a few growers use some Chardonnay in their still Pinot Blanc blends, but would never admit doing it. It always goes officially into the Crémant," says Olivier Humbrecht of Zind-Humbrecht.

So the composition and quality of "Pinot Blanc" are rather unpredictable. "Chardonnay was not admitted in the AOC category, mostly for political reasons, I think, not quality," says Olivier, whose 'Zind' cuvée (a Vin de France) gives a good indication of what Chardonnay can achieve in Alsace. Coming from the top Windsbuhl vineyard, it shows the character of terroir as much as the variety.

Muscat can in principle be intensely grapey, but is a mixed bag in Alsace as there are plantings of two types of Muscat. Muscat Blanc à Petit Grains (referred to locally as Muscat d'Alsace) is the highest quality cul-

Grape Varieties in Capsule

Sylvaner is a workhorse grape, not a great deal of character, mostly rather neutral in flavor. Occasionally an old vines cuvée shows more character. Not allowed in grand crus except for Zotzenberg, where it is a majority of plantings.

Auxerrois is often blended with Pinot Blanc, and labeled as Pinot Blanc, it tends to have a somewhat flat aromatic profile. It can show a more savory character from very old vines. Not allowed in grand crus.

Pinot Blanc is a higher quality than Auxerrois, but it's hard to find wines that are genuinely 100% varietal. Not allowed in grand crus.

Muscat is the only variety to show the smell of the grapes in the wine, which is usually quite perfumed; dry versions can seem austere because of the perfumed finish. They are fond of saying in Alsace that it's the perfect grape to match with asparagus (which kills many white wines).

Gewürztraminer is the most perfumed grape in Alsace, typically showing roses on the nose and lychees on the palate. Almost always off-dry or sweet to counteract its natural intrinsic bitterness on the finish. Low acidity enhances the sense of richness. Produces its best results to the south of Colmar in the Vallée Noble (south from Rouffach).

Klevener is a rosé variant of Traminer (the parent of Gewürztraminer) grown only around Heiligenstein and neighboring villages in the north. (It's not the same as Klevner or Clevner, which is an alternative name for Pinot Blanc). It's usually vinified in off-dry or sweet styles. It is not as exuberant or spicy as Gewürztraminer.

Pinot Gris is the only other grape with a range equivalent to Riesling, from dry to sweet, and often off-dry from grand crus. Flavors can range from spicy stone fruits tending to apricots, to a savory palate with impressions of fresh-cut mushrooms.

Riesling is without question, the greatest grape of Alsace, very reflective of terroir.

Pinot Noir represents the greatest change in Alsace in twenty years, from a pale style close to rosé to more deeply colored and extracted red wines. The best Pinot Noirs often come from plots in grand crus, although the grand cru cannot be identified on the label, but there are proposals to allow some grand crus to state Pinot Noir.

tivar in the Muscat family. Muscat Ottonel is much lower quality; in fact, it is not really Muscat as such, but is a cross between Muscat and Chasselas. Wines labeled as Muscat are usually a blend of both (even in the grand crus), so quality is rather variable. Alsace's quality wines therefore come from Pinot Gris, Gewürztraminer, and Riesling.

Pinot Gris reaches its full height of expression in Alsace; certainly it bears no resemblance at all to Pinot Grigio, the expression of the same variety in Italy. It's grown scarcely anywhere else in France. Although it is

Reference Wines for Dry White Alsace AOP	
Chardonnay (Vin de France)	Zind-Humbrecht, Zind
Sylvaner	Paul Blanck, Vieilles Vignes René Muré, Steinstuck Paul Kubler, La Petite Tête au Soleil Lucas Rieffel, Zotzenberg Dirler-Cadé, Vieilles Vignes
Auxerrois	Josmeyer, "H" Vieilles Vignes Paul Blanck, Alsace
Pinot Blanc	Marc Tempé, Zellenberg
Muscat	Domaine Ostertag, Fronholz Domaine Weinbach, Alsace Reserve Albert Mann, Alsace Reserve
Pinot Gris	Josmeyer, La Fromenteau Louis Sipp, Trottacker Albert Mann, Cuvée Albert
Gewürztraminer (usually off-dry)	Rolly Gassmann, Rorschwihr Domaine Weinbach, Altenbourg Zind-Humbrecht, Clos Windsbuhl
Riesling	Valentin Zusslin, Liebenberg Meyer Fonné, Pfoeller Marc Tempé, Grafenreben Louis Sipp, Hagel Domaine Josmeyer, Le Kottabe Paul Blanck, Rosenbourg

a variant of Pinot Noir, with skin varying in color intensity, it is vinified as a white wine and its aromatic profile is different. I wouldn't go so far as to call its character blowsy, but it has relatively low acidity, and with some rare exceptions, tends to have broad, soft flavors, sometimes with an oily texture, showing stone fruits tending to apricots; but it can also move in a more savory direction, sometimes veering towards suggestions of mushrooms. Old wines, approaching twenty years of age, can show truffles.

The big issue with Pinot Gris is that it really reaches ripeness only at high alcohol levels, so usually fermentation stops before completion, leaving some residual sugar. "It's complicated to make a dry Pinot Gris," is the way Céline Meyer at Domaine Josmeyer puts it. Residual sugar may be fairly minimal for wines labeled as Alsace AOP, but most grand cru Pinot Gris is perceptibly sweet. It also makes a fine late harvest wine, where those notes of mushrooms, accentuated by botrytis, can add complexity to the sweet apricot fruits.

Gewürz is German for spice, but Gewürztraminer is usually more perfumed than spicy. It is by far the most aromatic variety of Alsace, with a typical scent of roses on the nose; lychee fruits are characteristic on the palate. The classic description of Gewürztraminer is that it smells sweet but tastes dry, although this is not really true in Alsace. Those aromas of roses can turn quite phenolic on the finish and give a drying impression, but usually there is enough residual sugar to show perceptible sweetness. "Gewürztraminer needs a little sugar to counteract its intrinsic bitterness," says Catherine Faller at Domaine Weinbach. Even with

Vinification of white wines traditionally took place in foudres (large oval wooden casks), but many producers now use stainless steel.

some residual sugar, the alcohol level is often higher than other varieties. Gewürztraminer is a mainstay of the late harvest wines, with peaches and apricots joining lychees in Vendange Tardive, and botrytized flavors hiding the usual perfume at the level of Selection de Grains Nobles.

Virtually all high quality wine in Alsace is monovarietal. Marcel Deiss is probably the only producer who blends his top wines. When I asked Jean-Michel Deiss if he uses all seven varieties of Alsace he said, "Yes, all thirteen varieties!" There are the principal varieties such as Riesling (more than half of his plantings), then some secondary varieties (about a third), and finally, less than 10%, there are some old varieties that he is trying to preserve from disappearing.

Jean-Michel is quick to point out that he does not produce his wines by assemblage, the mixing of wines made from different varieties, but each is a single wine produced from grapes of different varieties intermingled in the vineyard. "I don't make wines to express the cépage, but to express the terroir," he says. He believes that to express terroir you need to grow varieties together. But this is distinctly a minority view.

Because the emphasis in Alsace is on aromatic varieties, there is usually no malolactic fermentation, which would introduce creamy notes clashing with varietal character (as well as reducing acidity in Pinot Gris and Gewürztraminer, which are already low acid varieties). So alcoholic fermentation is followed directly by a period of maturation. Fermentation in the traditional foudres is still used for top wines, but these days most wines are fermented in temperature-controlled stainless steel.

Maturation usually lasts a few months for entry-level wines; top wines are most often bottled just before the next harvest. "In Burgundy they talk about négociant-éleveurs but they don't exist in Alsace because we don't have élevage," says Marc Tempé, who is one of the few producers to break with tradition and use extended élevage in barriques. With rare exceptions, protracted maturation is not part of the style in Alsace.

Riesling

Riesling is the glory of Alsace, appearing in all styles from completely dry to totally botrytized. None of the other varieties can compete with its purity of flavors. When completely dry it can be steely and mineral, sometimes even saline. Fruits remain in the citrus spectrum. Riesling offers producers more of a choice than Pinot Gris or Gewürztraminer in determining style, because it ripens at lower alcohol levels. Because Riesling ripens more slowly, it is less prominent among the late harvest styles than Pinot Gris or Gewürztraminer.

Grown all over Alsace, Riesling is considered to be a "terroir grape," one that reflects its place more than most, making racy and elegant wines, always marked by fresh acidity. Many consider that the most striking results are obtained on granite, which emphasizes its steely minerality as a dry wine. In the sweet styles of Vendange Tardive or Selection de Grains Noble, Riesling still shows its piercing purity.

Riesling shows the playoff between sugar and acidity. When the high acidity has been ameliorated by a little residual sugar, it's an education to taste a series of wines and try to guess sugar and acidity levels: the interplay is so subtle that it's extremely difficult simply to place the wines in order of ascending residual sugar.

The most controversial aspect of Riesling is its tendency to develop an aroma of petrol with age. Opinion is divided as whether this is the essential character of Riesling or a flaw. It results from the production of TDN (trimethyl-dihydronaphthalene), which is rarely found in grapes but develops in the bottle by slow chemical actions. There are some misinformed opinions that this is caused by unripe grapes, but in fact, TDN levels are increased by low yields, warm weather, and high acidity.

Petrol never used to be noticeable before a wine had achieved several years of bottle age, but now it is more common in younger wines, presumably due to the effects of global warming. There is a research project to breed a cultivar of Riesling without the propensity to make TDN, but (in my opinion) this would destroy the typicity of the variety.

How does Riesling from Alsace differ from Riesling from elsewhere? The most immediate comparison is with Germany, just across the border to the north. Both Alsace and Germany show styles from dry to sweet, but Alsace divides its wines more clearly into dry/off-dry versus late-harvest dessert wines, while Germany has a complete range in between.

At the dry end of the scale, Alsace shows the result of its more southern location, which means that the growing cycle occurs earlier in the season, so the wines tend to be a little broader and richer; acidity and minerality are less obvious than those of the Mosel or Rheingau in Germany. There is greater variety of terroirs in Alsace, and a correspondingly broader range of styles.

Riesling from Austria is more like Germany than Alsace: the best wines tend to have a dry textured impression. There is the same lack of distinction between wines that are bone dry from those that taste more or less dry but actually have a little residual sugar: this is a feature of Riesling everywhere in Europe. Indeed, you might ask whether it is completely unfair to say that the main determinant of style is more whether any sugar left in the wine than differences in terroir.

New World Riesling, as typified by Australia, is quite different. Dry, with crushing acidity, the fruits tend to be more overtly citrus-driven, and can be quite aggressive.

The Alsace Appellation

With only two levels in the appellation hierarchy, Alsace AOP and Alsace Grand Cru, the appellation system in Alsace has been one of the least informative in France. Representing the vast majority of production, the Alsace AOP covers a range from innocuous entry-level wines to cuvées close to grand crus. Vineyards extend from the slopes of the Vosges mountains into the Plaine d'Alsace.

A giant depression runs all the way from the Vosges mountains at the west to the Black Forest in Germany at the east. This has filled with water over several geological periods, creating very fertile soils on the Plaine d'Alsace. The wines that come from here are the typical varietals of Alsace, many from large negociants, but the best that can be said about them is that they are ordinary.

Terroirs are quite varied, because two parallel geological faults stretch from north to south all along the Vosges and have thrown up many different soil formations. Soil types can change as frequently as every hundred meters. Limestone terroirs are common and include marl (compact mud and rock including clay and limestone), calcareous sandstone, and muschelkalk (sedimentary rock including limestone), but there are also granite terroirs and even volcanic around Thann, and some schist around Andlau, as well as other terroirs with low calcareous content.

A Hierarchy for Alsace AOP?

A change in the rules came into effect with the 2011 vintage to allow wines to be labeled with one of thirteen communal names or the name of a lieu-dit. The communal wines are usually blends from multiple plots around the village, while the lieu-dits are effectively single-vineyard wines. Using a lieu-dit involves some additional restrictions on plantings, and yields must be reduced to 68 hl/ha.

The use of lieu-dit and communal names anticipates a proposal to create a more hierarchical appellation structure, including premier crus and perhaps village wines. Even before the rules were changed, some producers were labeling single vineyard wines with the names of lieu-dits that they hope will become premier crus; and whether the system allows it or not, village names are being used for wines from around a village. Quality producers have eagerly seized on the idea, to the point at which most quality wines now have a name on the label.

(Most of the communal names do not have much meaning for the consumer: Bergheim, Blienschwiller, Saint-Hippolyte, Côtes de Barr Scherwiller, Côte de Rouffach, Côteaux du Haut Koenigsbourg, Vallée Noble, Klevener de Heiligenstein, Val Saint-Grégoire, Ottrott, Wolxheim, Rodern. Village names are more recognizable.)

Whether a formal hierarchical appellation system is approved or not, Alsace has effectively moved to a de facto hierarchy of the generic Alsace AOP, communal or village names, lieu-dits, and grand crus. This is a definite advance, although it is a bit undercut by the fact that the first three categories share the Alsace AOP. This can be confusing. as the labels for all levels appear similar, with the name, whether it is a brand, village, lieu-dit, or grand cru in large letters on the front, and you have to read the small print on the back label to work out a wine's position in the hierarchy. But if it's a grand cru, the label states AOP Alsace Grand Cru.

Premier cru is the name of the game in Alsace today. Hoping that INAO will approve a formal hierarchy, producers even sometimes openly describe their lieu-dits as candidates for promotion to premier cru. The proposed regulations for premier cru imply a quality level close to grand cru, for example, with yields limited to 57 hl/ha.

This will not eliminate a surreal element in the present system. "Some premier cru wines may sell at higher prices than some grand cru wines," says Céline Meyer at Domaine Josmeyer, recognizing that premier crus are likely to be defined with greater consistency, whereas grand crus remain extremely variable. Could any grand crus be demoted? "No, there is no willingness to open the grand cru box. The system is not perfect but it exists. It's much more important to organize a classification of the intermediate levels," says Étienne Sipp at Domaine Louis Sipp.

There's talk that there might be as many as 160 premier crus, so it's a concern whether the system will become so complicated as to confuse the consumer, especially given that it can be difficult to distinguish the Germanic names. I am afraid that the system will lack credibility unless the variability of the grand crus is taken in hand at the same time.

A weakness of the present system is that not all of the grand crus have really achieved reputations in their own right. Sometimes a grand cru is associated with a single wine from a particular producer, rather than from several producers, so it's really the wine and producer that have the reputation rather than the grand cru as such. "It's important that a lieu-dit or premier cru should be represented by multiple producers so it doesn't just have one style," Jean-Christophe Bott argues.

The Grand Crus

All the wines of interest come from the west, where the villages on the Route du Vin are mostly huddled under the Vosges, and producers who make wines from the slopes are somewhat disdainful about wines coming from the plain. The Grand Crus lie on either side of the western fault, dispersed the full length of the appellation.

It is no coincidence that most of the villages on the Route des Vins have a single grand cru associated with them. Each village proposed its best vineyards for grand cru status, and some sort of liberté, égalité, fraternité resulted, with most villages getting one, and only one, grand cru. Often enough, it's the steepest hill near the village.

Grand Crus were controversial when they were introduced, and acceptance of the system was slow. The lack of any hierarchy in the initial classification system—all AOP wines were originally described simply as Vins d'Alsace—led to the establishment of a committee in the 1970s to consider the promotion of the best vineyards to higher status. But the results were so controversial that several of the most important producers refused to use the system.

The basic problem was that in order to get the system approved, too many grand crus were created, and many of them are much too large. The first one set the pattern. The hill of Schlossberg lies between the Kaysersberg and the town of Kintzheim, avowedly including some of the best terroir in Alsace. The original committee recommended it should include a total area of about 25 ha, but as finally approved it consists of about 80 ha: politics triumphed over geology.

There's no consistent system for organizing grand crus: most stand alone, but sometimes two or three run right into one another, and sometimes a grand cru consists of several separated parts. Defenders would say this represents the lie of the terroir, critics that politics has been more important than geography. It's fair to say that the grand crus do include most of the best sites in Alsace, but the political nature of the process makes the label unreliable as an indication of the very best quality. "Johnny Hugel (who chaired the first committee) wanted to define the best of the best, but his peers didn't understand that there would be problems years later if you expanded the grand crus," says Marc Hugel. The Hugels believe that the whole concept has been devalued, and so far have refused to use the names of grand crus.

"There are too many grand crus in Alsace, and the size of some of them is just too big. Also the yields in grand crus are too high. More than half of grand cru juice goes to cooperatives, who have no idea what to do with it, so you can find grand cru wines in supermarkets at (low) prices that are simply criminal," says Hubert Trimbach. And there's a serious lack of consistency. "It's not the number of grand crus that's the issue but the delimitation. Some of the tops and bottoms of hills should perhaps be premier cru," says Felix Meyer at Meyer-Fonné.

15

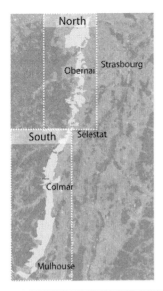

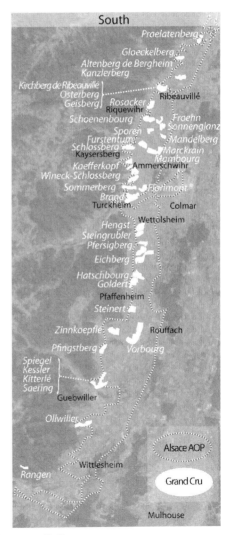

Grand crus extend the length of the Alsace appellation.

Grand Crus in Alsace are often the most elevated sites near each village. Kitterlé rises up steeply immediately above the town of Guebwiller.

By the time you add up the top wines from Trimbach, Hugel (the major owner of the grand crus Sporen and Schoenenbourg), and Léon Beyer (another top producer who does not use the grand cru system), a significant proportion of grand crus have been deprived of recognition. However, hostility to the grand crus is softening: Trimbach introduced their first grand cru label (Geisberg), and Hugel introduced Schoelhammer, named for a plot in Schoenenbourg, both in 2015.

Grand crus overall are known as much for extra richness and (sometimes) for higher quality than for specific styles. They include all types of terroirs. Among the granite grand crus, Brand is taut, Schlossberg gives precision, and Sommerberg has grip. Because water retention is poor, the warm granite terroirs such as Brand (which means brûlé or burning) and Schlossberg may not do their best in the warmest years, when Sommerberg and Winneck-Schlossberg may do better. The calcareous muschelkalk of Rosacker (including Clos St. Hune) tends to tension, while other calcareous terroirs, such as Furstentum and Altenberg de Bergheim, tend more to delicacy and to elegance. Limestone-rich marl, such as Sonnenglanz, tend towards power. Terroirs with marl and calcareous sandstone include the austerity of Schoenenbourg, the upright minerality of Osterberg, and Pfersigberg. The marl of Geisberg and Sporen tends to opulence, and in Hengst to power.

Grand Cru Schoenenbourg rises up immediately outside the town walls of Riquewihr.

It is by no means true that Riesling is necessarily the top variety in each grand cru. Gewürztraminer does especially well in the warm Vallée Noble to the south of Rouffach, and is by far the dominant variety in the Zinnkoepflé grand cru (the name means heads in the sun in local dialect). Grand cru Goldert ripens late, and so is especially suitable for late harvest wines, where again Gewürztraminer is dominant. On the volcanic terroir of Rangen, Pinot Gris is the top variety. And Zotzenberg is the only grand cru that admits Sylvaner. If Pinot Noir is allowed to be labeled as grand cru, there may be other notable exceptions in the future.

Grand cru wines are almost all monovarietals (blends are allowed only in Altenberg de Bergheim and Kaefferkopf). Plantings do somewhat represent which varieties do best in which grand cru, but there are no legal restrictions, so that any of the four permitted varieties can be grown in any of the grand crus. Overall, Riesling and Gewürztraminer each occupy roughly 40% of total plantings in grand crus, with Pinot Gris representing about 20%. Muscat is almost insignificant; in fact, given that the best Pinot Noirs in Alsace come from plots in grand crus, there may actually be more Pinot Noir than Muscat planted in grand crus.

So far, there's no proposal that premier crus (if they are created) might be specific for certain varieties or that grand crus might have restrictions to specific grape varieties. But isn't the essence of the French concept of terroir that there are specific matches between each terroir and certain grape varieties? Indeed, Philippe Kubler at Domaine Paul Kubler says that, "I think the project for my generation should be to make each grand cru represent only one cépage. We know that Zinnkoepflé is superb for Gewürztraminer, but maybe not for Riesling. And Schlossberg is great for Riesling, but maybe not for Gewürztraminer."

Alsace Grand Crus			
Cru	*Village(s)*	*Hectares*	*Created*
Altenberg de Bergbieten	Bergbieten	29	1983
Altenberg de Bergheim	Bergheim	35	1983
Altenberg de Wolxheim	Wolxheim	31	1992
Brand	Turckheim	58	1983
Bruderthal	Molsheim	18	1992
Eichberg	Eguisheim	58	1983
Engelberg	Dahlenheim, Scharrachbergheim	15	1992
Florimont	Ingersheim, Katzenthal	21	1992
Frankstein	Dambach-la-Ville	56	1992
Froehn	Zellenberg	15	1992
Furstentum	Kientzheim, Sigolsheim	31	1992
Geisberg	Ribeauvillé	9	1983
Gloeckelberg	Rodern, Saint-Hippolyte	23	1983
Goldert	Gueberschwihr	45	1983
Hatschbourg	Hattstatt, Voegtlinshoffen	47	1983
Hengst	Wintzenheim	76	1983
Kaefferkopf	Ammerschwihr	72	2007
Kanzlerberg	Bergheim	3	1983
Kastelberg	Andlau	6	1983
Kessler	Guebwiller	29	1983
Kirchberg de Barr	Barr	41	1983
Kirchberg de Ribeauvillé	Ribeauvillé	11	1983
Kitterlé	Guebwiller	26	1983
Mambourg	Sigolsheim	62	1992
Mandelberg	Mittelwihr, Beblenheim	22	1992
Marckrain	Bennwihr, Sigolsheim	53	1992
Moenchberg	Andlau, Eichhoffen	12	1983
Muenchberg	Nothalten	18	1992
Ollwiller	Wuenheim	36	1983
Osterberg	Ribeauvillé	25	1992
Pfersigberg	Eguisheim, Wettolsheim	75	1992
Pfingstberg	Orschwihr	28	1992
Praelatenberg	Kintzheim	19	1992
Rangen	Thann, Vieux-Thann	22	1983
Rosacker	Hunawihr	26	1983
Saering	Guebwiller	27	1983
Schlossberg	Kientzheim	80	1975
Schoenenbourg	Riquewihr, Zellenberg	53	1992
Sommerberg	Niedermorschwihr, Katzenthal	28	1983
Sonnenglanz	Beblenheim	33	1983
Spiegel	Bergholtz, Guebwiller	18	1983
Sporen	Riquewihr	24	1992
Steinert	Pfaffenheim, Westhalten	39	1992
Steingrubler	Wettolsheim	23	1992
Steinklotz	Marlenheim	41	1992
Vorbourg	Rouffach, Westhalten	74	1992
Wiebelsberg	Andlau	13	1983
Wineck-Schlossberg	Katzenthal, Ammerschwihr	27	1992
Winzenberg	Blienschwiller	19	1992
Zinnkoepflé	Soultzmatt, Westhalten	71	1992
Zotzenberg	Mittelbergheim	36	1992

The Top Grand Crus			
Cru	Soil Type	Wine Character	Predominant Varieties
Brand	south-facing granite and black mica, very poor soil, warm microclimate	taut & elegant	Riesling Gewürztraminer Pinot Gris
Eichberg	southeast-facing calcareous and siliceous pebbles	full-bodied & round	Gewürztraminer Riesling Pinot Gris
Furstentum	brown, pebbly, limestone and sandstone	delicate & aromatic	Riesling Gewürztraminer
Geisberg	calcareous sandstone and marl	rich & opulent	Riesling
Goldert	east-southeast-facing limestone pebbles and sandstone on limestone substratum	late ripening gives richness, often dessert wines	Gewürztraminer
Hengst	east-facing brown marl, limestone, and sandstone	powerful & austere	Gewürztraminer Pinot Gris
Osterberg	south-southeast-facing, calcareous	linear & mineral	Riesling
Pfingstberg	marl, limestone, sandstone	savory & herbal	Riesling
Rangen	volcanic	tension	Riesling Gewürztraminer
Rosacker	muschelkalk (calcareous)	tension	Pinot Gris Riesling
Schlossberg	south-facing granite	precise	Riesling
Schoenenbourg	marl, rock, and gypsum	delicate, precise, austere	Riesling
Sommerberg	south-facing granite	tension	Riesling
Sonnenglanz	southeast-facing marl and limestone	spicy to exotic	Pinot Gris Gewürztraminer
Sporen	southeast-facing clay-marl	opulent	Gewürztraminer Pinot Gris
Vorbourg	south-southeast-facing limestone and sandstone	steely & mineral	Gewürztraminer (Pinot Noir)
Zinnkoepflé	south-facing muschelkalk (calcareous) at 260-430m	rich but with freshness	Gewürztraminer

Reference Wines for Grand Cru: Riesling	
Altenbourg	Domaine Loew
Brand	Josmeyer
Eichberg	"R" de Beyer*
Furstentum	Paul Blanck
Geisberg	Trimbach
Goldert	Ernest Burn, Clos St. Imer La Chapelle
Hengst	Josmeyer
Herrenweg de Turckheim	Zind-Humbrecht
Kaefferkopf	Jean-Baptiste Adam Meyer-Fonné
Kastelberg	Marc Kreydenweiss
Kirchberg de Ribeauvillé	Louis Sipp
Kitterlé	Domaine Schlumberger
Mandelberg	Bott-Geyl
Muenchberg	Domaine Ostertag
Osterberg	Louis Sipp
Pfersigberg	Léon Beyer, Comtes d'Eguisheim* Léon Beyer, Les Ecaillers*
Pfingstberg	Valentin Zusslin
Rangen (Clos St. Urbain)	Zind-Humbrecht
Rosacker	Trimbach, Clos Sainte Hune*
Saering	Domaine Schlumberger
Schlossberg	Domaine Weinbach, Cuvée St. Catherine
Schoenenbourg	Hugel, Jubilee* Hugel, Schoelhammer*
Sommerberg	Paul Blanck Domaine Schoffit
Wineck-Schlossberg	Meyer-Fonné
Vorbourg	René Muré, Clos St. Landelin
Geisberg/Osterberg	Trimbach, Frédéric Emile*

Grand cru is not stated on label, which shows only Alsace AOP

Reference Wines for Grand Cru: Gewürztraminer & Pinot Gris

Gewürztraminer

Eichberg	Jean-Louis & Fabienne Mann
Furstentum	Albert Mann Weinbach Zind Humbrecht
Hatschbourg	Joseph Cattin
Hengst	Josmeyer
Kessler	Schlumberger
Mambourg	Marc Tempé
Osterberg	Sipp Mack
Pfersigberg	Paul Ginglinger
Pfingstberg	François Schmitt
Saering	Dirler-Cade
Sonnenglanz	Bott-Geyl
Sporen (Grossi Laüe*)	Hugel & Fils Meyer-Fonné
Steingrubler	Albert Mann Barmès-Buecher
Vorbourg	René Muré, Clos St. Landelin
Zinnkoepflé	Léon Boesch Paul Kubler

Pinot Gris

Eichberg	Paul Ginglinger
Furstentum	Paul Blanck
Hengst	Josmeyer
Muenchberg	Marc Kreydenweiss
Rangen de Thann (Clos St. Théobald)	Schoffit
Rosacker	Sipp Mack
Rosenberg	Albert Mann Barmès-Buecher
Schoenenbourg	Marc Tempé
Schlossberg (Cuvée Sainte Catherine)	Weinberg
Zinnkoepflé	Paul Kubler

While some grand crus have been recognized as superior to other sites, they represent only a handful of examples. It may need the introduction of premier crus to achieve the same general focus as in other areas of France on the relationships between terroir and grape varieties.

Sweetness in Alsace

Sugar is the word that cannot speak its name in Alsace. Indeed, wine production is bedeviled by the issue of sweetness, and the major single factor that has held Alsace back from better success in the market is probably the unpredictable level of sweetness in its wines. "When I started 35 years ago, almost all wines had less than 3 grams residual sugar. Now most wines have more. I think there is a relation between the fact that Alsace has placed itself with sweet wines and the fact that prices have stayed low. One problem is that every other region has regulations for alcohol levels and sweetness but Alsace does not," says Marc Hugel. "Our image as a dry-wine region is at risk," Étienne Hugel commented.

There are two conflicting trends in Alsace today. One is a demand for dry wines to go with food; younger producers especially are trying to make wines in a drier style than their parents. The other is that sugar levels at harvest have been pushed up by warmer vintages, so there's a trend to leave some residual sugar in the wine because producers feel that alcohol would be too high if fermentation went to completion. Even producers who consider that sweetness is a problem concede that there are benefits. "I would say that in Alsace global warming has increased enormously the quality of the wine, even if it has brought the problem of residual sugar," Marc Hugel allows. Sometimes there are suspicions that producers are stopping fermentation to make the wines more crowd-pleasing, but Jean Boxler at Domaine Albert Boxler says that, "We have more problems in continuing fermentation than in stopping it at a specific sweetness."

Some producers believe that wine should always be dry. "Our wine is bone-dry and therefore suitable to accompany food," says Hubert Trimbach. Other notable houses in this camp are Hugel, Josmeyer, and Beyer. But what is dry? A wine will always taste dry if it has less than 4 g/l residual sugar (this is the usual limit for calling a wine dry), but it may taste virtually dry if it has high enough acidity, even if it is over 4 g/l residual sugar. Some wines may start out with a little residual sugar, but will taste dry by the time they are ready to drink. Marc Hugel, who is completely committed to the dry style, says, "It's a mystery why sweet wine tastes drier as it ages. If there is high potential alcohol, sometimes I prefer to leave a little residual sugar, but by the time we market the wine, 6-7 years later, it tastes dry."

Achieving a dry balance is more difficult with Pinot Gris and Gewürztraminer than

Reference Producers Committed to a Dry Style

Laurent Barth
Charles Baur
Léon Beyer
Léon Boesch
Henry Fuchs
Maison Hugel
Domaine Josmeyer
Jean-Luc Mader
Jean-Louis & Fabienne Mann
René Muré
Pierre et Jean-Pierre Rietsch
Domaine Pfister
Martin Schaetzel
François Schmitt
Maison Trimbach
Domaine Weinbach

with Riesling. Statistically speaking, if you select a Riesling from Alsace from an unknown producer, you have a good chance of it being dry or almost dry, but Pinot Gris is often off-dry, and Gewürztraminer will almost always be at least a little sweet. This is partly because these varieties reach phenolic ripeness only at higher sugar levels, and partly because they have lower acidity that makes any residual sugar more obvious.

The issue of sweetness is tied up with the grand cru system, because the grand crus were defined at a time when getting to ripeness was problematic. So they are the sites that achieve greatest ripeness, often south-facing hillsides. An outdated regulation requires potential alcohol to reach 10% at harvest, but today it's more of a problem to restrain alcohol. In a typical vintage when the grand crus were defined, the distinction might have been that a grand cru reached an acceptable level of alcohol naturally, whereas an AOC Alsace vineyard needed chaptalization.

So the wines would have the same (dry) style, but the grand cru would display the extra character that goes with greater ripeness. In the present era of warmer vintages, however, the appellation vineyard may reach an acceptable level of potential alcohol, and the grand cru may rise above it. This explains why at many producers the entry-level wine is always fermented to dryness, but the grand crus show some residual sugar.

The argument is basically that something has to give: either alcohol will be too high or there will be residual sugar. This might not be so much of an issue if the style was consistent for any given producer and stayed the same between vintages. Vintage variation is a problem when a wine is dry in one vintage and sweet in another. And it's equally confusing when a producer changes style from AOP Alsace to grand cru. "The problem is not with the entry-level, it's more with the grand crus, where the Riesling may be picked at 14% potential alcohol. It's more difficult to achieve dry Riesling and we can find grand crus with 7-8 g/l sugar or more; it's totally stupid for the grand crus to have residual sugar," says Pierre Trimbach.

In my view, this is spot on as a criticism, because it is impossible to appreciate the difference between an appellation Riesling and a grand cru Riesling if the first is dry and the second is sweet. I should admit to a prejudice here that you can't really appreciate nuances of terroir when the palate is muddied by residual sugar. So at some producers, the most interesting wines are the middle of the range, because the basic wines are too simple, but the grand crus are too sweet.

Even the most committed producers admit that it's mostly impossible (and maybe undesirable) to get completely dry Pinot Gris or Gewürztraminer from grand crus. "Pinot Gris ripens very rapidly. Sometimes you say you harvest in the morning and it's dry, you harvest in the afternoon and it's sweet," says Étienne Sipp. "Gewürztraminer will reach 13-14% when Riesling gets to 11%," Marc Hugel says, conceding, "It's better to have 14% alcohol and 7 g/l sugar than 15% alcohol and bone dry." And Céline Meyer at Domaine Josmeyer points out that, "If Gewürztraminer is completely dry it's not agreeable because it's too bitter."

The consensus is that, faute de mieux, Gewürztraminer (and Pinot Gris) are going to have some sugar. "I prefer to make dry wines and for Riesling it's easy to be dry, but with the grand crus for Pinot Gris and Gewürztraminer we cannot produce dry wines. To follow what the terroir has to give you, the wine would not be balanced if you picked early enough to make dry wine," says Jean-Christophe Bott. But he adds ruefully, "Of course the market is looking for dry wine." The best you can do with Pinot Gris and Gewürztraminer is usually to produce a wine that tastes very nearly dry.

Alongside the issue of sugar, is the question of botrytis. While botrytis is desirable in late harvest wines, producers differ on whether they welcome it in dry (or nearly dry) wines, but it's not uncommon, especially at the grand cru level, to have a small proportion of botrytized grapes. Indeed, at Meyer Fonné, Felix Meyer only makes SGN where there's enough botrytis not to deprive the grand cru: "In most years there's 15% or so in the grand cru Gewürztraminer, and I don't want to take that out, it's part of the character," he says.

Sec	d'esprit	demi-sec	moeulleux	liquoreux
	Sec			

1   2   3   4   5

1	2	3	4	5	6	7	8	9

<Sec/Dry   Liquoreux/Sweet>

Two scales used on Alsace back labels rate sweetness by 5 or 9 points. The first three points usually indicate dry, off-dry, and medium sweet.

At Domaine Paul Blanck, Frédéric Blanck takes a different view: "I don't want to see botrytis in the classic (entry-level) range because it changes the flavor of everything. Botrytis is perfect in late harvest but has nothing to do with grand cru because you can get concentration without it, and we want to see the purity." You can make delicious wine with or without botrytis; it's really a matter of whether you regard it as a feature of terroir or as a complication.

One of the biggest problems for the consumer has been the failure to come to terms with sugar levels: unless a wine is Vendange Tardive or SGN, there is no official way to know whether it is dry or off-dry. When he was president of the CIVA (the local wine organization), Rémy Gresser acknowledged that "When consumers buy Sancerre, they know it's a dry white wine, but with Alsatian wines, they don't know what they'll find in the bottle." He thought the problem started with a knock-on effect from the official recognition of sweet late-harvest wines in the 1980s.

Producers have finally realized that this is a major impediment in the marketplace, and have introduced a scale of sweetness on the back label. Étienne Hugel was against the idea because "it means we have lost the battle," and it's fair to say that it may help to resolve uncertainty, but at the cost of reinforcing the image that wine from Alsace is not reliably dry. However, it is no more than a partial solution, because information on the back label is not evident on, for example, a restaurant wine list; and furthermore the scale is neither consistent nor objective. Some producers use a 5 point scale, some use a 9 point scale.

Actually, I do not think either scale has much significance beyond the first three points, because once a wine is sweet, it is sweet, and it would be a rare person who would choose it on the basis of just how sweet. The critical point is whether a wine tastes bone dry, or what I call ambiguously dry (when you don't think it's bone dry, but can't quite taste sweetness), or distinctly off-dry.

Aside from that, the problem is that right at the most sensitive point of the scale, the difference between bone-dry and off-dry, most producers are assigning #1 or #2 on the basis of taste. This is a mistake because sensitivities differ: indeed, when I've questioned whether a particular wine should really be #1, producers sometimes admit that the number depends on who is making the assignment that day. "The problem is that everyone has their own system, when I see what's on the label sometimes I'm astonished," says Marc Hugel. If even in Champagne they have started to put dosage levels on the label, why can't they put the level of residual sugar on the label in Alsace?

One solution would be for Alsace to indicate on the label when a wine is unambiguously dry. In 2016, with some dissent, an agreement was finally reached to use *Sec* on the label, but it has yet to be implemented. Unfortunately, however, the definition of Sec follows the mistaken view of the E.U. that a wine can be considered dry even when it has more than 4 g/l residual sugar, so long as it has sufficiently high acidity.

The basic idea is that high acidity hides the sweetness. This is true up to a point, but is subjective, as people differ in their ability to detect sweetness against a background of high acidity. While most of the wines labeled as Sec do taste bone dry, some do not, showing a slight sweetness. The sweetness scale now is used for wines that do not qualify as Sec. But none of this is going to work until producers accept that there is an international standard for bone-dry wine: less than 4 g/l of residual sugar.

Producers committed to the dry style feel that this should be the default. "As far as we are concerned, Alsace Riesling should be dry," says Emanuelle Gallis of the Cave de Turckheim "Off-dry or sweet should be the exception, so we'd prefer it if those who make those styles had to put that on their labels."

Orange wine is another style altogether, something of a fashion among committed "natural" wine producers, albeit on a limited basis. Basically an orange wine is made by treating white grapes like black grapes, and allowing skin contact during fermentation. How orange it gets depends on how long the skins macerate with the juice. Gewürztraminer is a prime candidate among producers who want to produce really dry wine, with leading examples from Laurent Bannwarth, Pierre Frick, and Domaine Trapet.

For all of the problems with sugar confusing the palate of supposedly dry wines, there is no argument about the quality of the sweet wines of Alsace. Vendange Tardive and Selection de Grains Nobles dessert wines have been classified separately in Alsace since 1984. Even here the classification refers to the sugar level at time of harvest rather than to residual sugar after fermentation; however, given the sugar levels at harvest, VT and SGN wines are always sweet.

Chaptalization cannot be used for VT or SGN wines; in fact, the regulations for their production are among the strictest in France for dessert wines. Their reputation is as high as for any sweet wine anywhere, but they represent only an average 1-2% of production, with amounts fluctuating widely from year to year according to vintage conditions.

"We cannot compete on price or varietal name. We are on steep slopes, we have high labor costs. Let's try to put our terroir into the bottle," says Étienne Sipp, expressing his view of the future for Alsace. The region has one of the great varieties in Riesling, which I think is possibly the most versatile white variety of all. There is a series of different terroirs at grand cru level where Riesling shows all the nuances of its range of expression as a dry wine. Pinot Gris and Gewürztraminer can show real varietal character in Alsace. The late harvest wines can achieve great purity and interest extending beyond mere sweetness.

It is a shame that uncertainty about wine styles, and failure to be strict enough about yields and to take the classification system in hand, have prevented the region from establishing the reputation it deserves.

Red Wine

The only black grape permitted in Alsace is Pinot Noir. Until recently, this was very definitely an also-ran, with most of the wines showing a resemblance to rosé. Global warming has changed things: producers are now taking red wine seriously. Have you always made Pinot Noir, I asked Étienne Sipp of Domaine Louis Sipp. "Yes, but not in the present way. There is a big change, people are rethinking Pinot Noir, they plant it in good places, they produce more concentrated wine."

It's a sign of how things have changed that at Hugel, who were probably first to make Pinot Noir in a Burgundian way when they started in 1977, winemaker Johnny Hugel said "If you force me to make Pinot Noir, I'll make vinegar," but today Marc Hugel makes very fine Pinot Noir. It's a mark of the change that whereas in the past, most producers have shown only white wines for tasting, on my most recent visit virtually every producer had a creditable red wine.

Progress even goes so far that Mathieu Boesch, at Domaine Léon Boesch towards the southern end of the wine region, can say that, "East-West facing is good for Pinot Noir as it's not too hot." A sign of the commitment to serious red wines is that many Pinot Noirs are made by

Reference Wines for Pinot Noir	
Burlenberg	Marcel Deiss
Les Neveux (lieu-dit Pflostig)	Maison Hugel
Grand H (Hengst)	Albert Mann
Chemin de Pierre	Jean-Louis & Fabienne Mann
"V" (Vorbourg grand cru)	René Muré
Runz	André & Lucas Rieffel
"M" (Mambourg grand cru)	Marc Tempé
"W" (Clos des Capucins)	Domaine Weinbach
Bollenberg Harmonie	Valentin Zusslin

vendange entière, when whole bunches go into the press, instead of removing the stems first. This requires a high degree of ripeness (as otherwise the stems introduce unripe tannins).

"The idea is not to copy Burgundy, but the Pinot comes from the most calcareous places in the vineyards. We want to produce something silky and elegant in Pinot Noir," says Jean-Christophe Bott of Domaine Bott-Geyl. The style in Alsace usually more resembles Côte de Beaune than Côte de Nuits, and tends to be soft, smooth, and earthy. The reds sometimes seem to show an aromatic spectrum relating to the fact that Alsace focuses on aromatic white varieties.

The best wines tend to come from calcareous areas of grand crus. Typically they are ready about five or six years after the vintage, but will hold as long again. The warming trend has definitely created a new opportunity for Alsace. "With the climate change, we probably now have the same climate in Alsace that Burgundy had twenty years ago," said Étienne Hugel.

The change has been recognized to the extent of proposing that Pinot Noir should be allowed to be labeled as grand cru if coming from the grand crus of Vorbourg, Hengst, and Kirchberg. It's a sign of the times that producers expect this proposal to succeed, whereas a similar one twenty years ago was turned down.

Vintages

Historically Alsace has alternated between good vintages and poor vintages, but the recent global warming trend has produced a run of good vintages, albeit with different characters. There's a marked difference between overtly rich vintages such as 2007, 2009, and 2015, and more "classical" vintages, such as 2010 or 2016, which have higher acidity, for example, providing a style for every taste.

2019	**	The heat wave was difficult for many producers, with yields reduced 30-40% from 2018, especially for Gewürztraminer, but rainfall in August and September helped, wines have good concentration. Riesling's natural high acidity helped it, and Pinot Noir should be very good.
2018	**	All the rain came early, with a year's worth in the first seven months, then a hot growing season, as all over France, gave round wines with lower acidity than usual, tending towards opulence. Hot and mostly dry summer, with hottest July since 1947, led to early harvest, with top results for Pinot Gris and Pinot Noir. There was good production of sweet wines following Indian summer.
2017	**	Spring frosts reduced yields about 20%, but mostly damaged vineyards on the flat: vineyards on grand crus and other hillsides were much less affected. Growing season was fifth hottest on record, with occasional rainfall, and both dry and sweet wines are very good.
2016	**	After three years of small yields, a normal vintage, with a late harvest. Regarded as classical for dry wines, and better than 2014 for dry and off-dry styles from the late-ripening varieties of Riesling, Pinot Gris, and Gewürztraminer, but few botrytized wines.
2015	***	Warm, dry season gave rich wines. Dry styles are often atypically rich, delicious but at the price of some blurring of the usual crisp focus. There are late harvest wines, and good Pinot Noirs.
2014	*	Cool August produced restrained dry whites with high acidity that may need time to calm down. Dry wines may be worth aging. There are few late harvest wines.
2013		Growing season was dry but not very sunny, then rain at harvest meant that early pickers did best. Wines tend to be light and acidity can be high. Few show much generosity. This is a vintage for early drinking.
2012	**	Warm August and cool September gave good results, with a classic balance of fruit to acidity. It was especially successful for Pinot Noir.
2011	*	Decent but not great vintage, generally giving a fresh, fruity style; not much in the way of late harvest wines. Dry wines should be drunk early.
2010	**	Very high acidity caused many wines to take time to come around. Riesling can still be piercing, but the best wines are fresh and pure with classic minerality, and should have longevity. There are few late harvest wines.
2009	***	Precocious vintage in rich style, with powerful Rieslings and opulent Pinot Gris and Gewürztraminer. Alcohol is high for dry wines, which are developing relatively fast.

2008	**	Generally cool season saved by Indian summer; the style is often restrained, and some wines were slow to open. Not as good as 2007 or 2009.
2007	***	Regarded as a great vintage all round, rich with even Riesling tending to opulence rather than minerality. Possibly the richest since 1997, with some great botrytized wines.
2006		A variable year, with rather heterogeneous results resulting from difficulties with getting to ripeness, but good acidity for Rieslings.
2005	**	Not such a good year in Alsace as elsewhere in France, with some problems reaching ripeness; grand crus are the most reliable.
2004	*	High yields resulted in lack of concentration. Rieslings performed best. There are few late harvest wines.
2003		The great heat of this vintage produced wines that matured early, although some of the reds have been very fine.
2002	*	Difficult year because of alternating hot and cold conditions, but the best wines had good structure and acidity, and sufficient ripeness.
2001	**	Poor and late start to season, recovery in August, then problems in September, but wines were harvested in October Indian summer, giving some exceptionally fine late harvest wines.
2000	*	An early start was followed by a favorable growing season, but there were heavy rains in October. Dry wines are good, if not outstanding, and there are even some late harvest wines.

Visiting the Region

Even though the Alsace wine region is long and skinny, most producers are within 20-30 minutes of Colmar, which is the major town in the region, but as this is a major tourist region there are hotels and restaurants all the way from Rouffach to Ribeauvillé. There are innumerable medieval villages, many with restaurants and accommodation. The town centers of the major tourist villages — Ribeauvillé,

The main street of Riquewihr is one of the sights of medieval Alsace.

Riquewihr, Kaysersberg, and Eguisheim—are closed to traffic, so it is necessary to park in the car parks on the outskirts. However, few producers are within the restricted areas.

Because Alsace is a major tourist area, most producers have tasting rooms that are open most days. But remember that the lunch hour is sacrosanct in France, and virtually all tasting rooms are closed between 12 p.m. and 2 p.m. It is a sign of changing times in France that some tasting rooms are now open at weekends. In some cases, in fact, the tasting room is open at the weekend, and an appointment is needed during the week, but usually an appointment is not needed.

Many of the producers on the Route du Vin are small family affairs, and you are likely to be greeted by a member of the family. Cellar door sales are important in Alsace, and it is usually possible to buy wines at the tasting room (indeed, the producer may be disappointed if you leave without making a purchase).

Tastings can be quite protracted, because even small producers tend to have a wide range of wines. Usually there is an entry-level wine for each grape variety under the Alsace AOP label; for each of the more important grape varieties there may be some village or single-vineyard wines; and very likely there will be two or three grand cru cuvées. In addition, there may be some Vendange

Petite Venise on the river is the heart of medieval Colmar.

Eguisheim is the most picturesque village south of Colmar.

High above the vineyards, Château Haut Koenigsbourg is one of the major sights of Alsace.

Tardive or SGN dessert wines. The list of wines can easily run to twenty or so.

Do not be surprised to be offered red wine first, followed by the whites—this is because the aromatics of the white wines can make it difficult to appreciate the Pinot Noir afterwards. In planning an itinerary, allow at least an hour for each visit, but going through the whole range is likely to take closer to two hours at most producers.

The etiquette of tasting assumes you will spit. A producer will be surprised if you drink the wine. Usually a tasting room or cellar is equipped with spittoons, but ask if you do not see one (crachoir in French). Of course, some tourists do enjoy drinking the wines, but producers will take you more seriously if you spit.

Maps

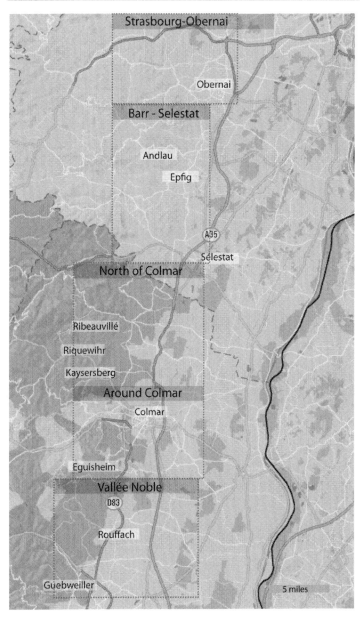

Strasbourg-Obernai

Obernai

Barr - Selestat

Andlau

Epfig

A35

Sélestat

North of Colmar

Ribeauvillé

Riquewihr

Kaysersberg

Around Colmar

Colmar

Eguisheim

Vallée Noble

D83

Rouffach

Guebweiller

5 miles

34

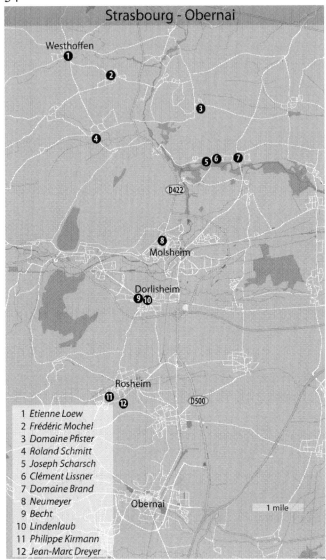

Strasbourg - Obernai

Westhoffen
1
2
3
4
5 6 7
D422
8
Molsheim
Dorlisheim
9 10
Rosheim
11 12
D500

1 *Etienne Loew*
2 *Frédéric Mochel*
3 *Domaine Pfister*
4 *Roland Schmitt*
5 *Joseph Scharsch*
6 *Clément Lissner*
7 *Domaine Brand*
8 *Neumeyer*
9 *Becht*
10 *Lindenlaub*
11 *Philippe Kirmann*
12 *Jean-Marc Dreyer*

Obernai

1 mile

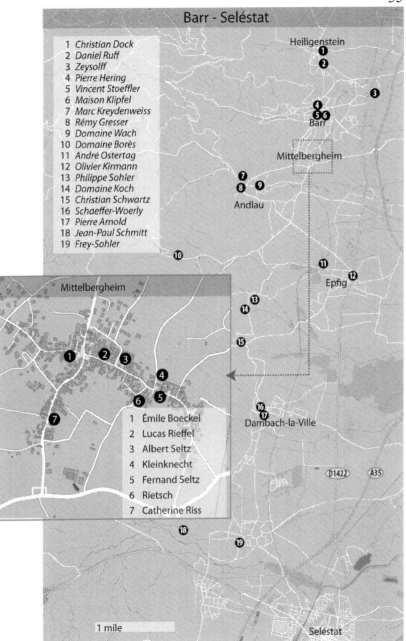

Barr - Seléstat

1 Christian Dock
2 Daniel Ruff
3 Zeysolff
4 Pierre Hering
5 Vincent Stoeffler
6 Maison Klipfel
7 Marc Kreydenweiss
8 Rémy Gresser
9 Domaine Wach
10 Domaine Borès
11 André Ostertag
12 Olivier Kirmann
13 Philippe Sohler
14 Domaine Koch
15 Christian Schwartz
16 Schaeffer-Woerly
17 Pierre Arnold
18 Jean-Paul Schmitt
19 Frey-Sohler

Heiligenstein

Barr

Mittelbergheim

Andlau

Epfig

Mittelbergheim

1 Émile Boeckel
2 Lucas Rieffel
3 Albert Seltz
4 Kleinknecht
5 Fernand Seltz
6 Rietsch
7 Catherine Riss

Dambach-la-Ville

D1422   A35

1 mile

Seléstat

North of Colmar: Rohrschwihr - Beblenheim

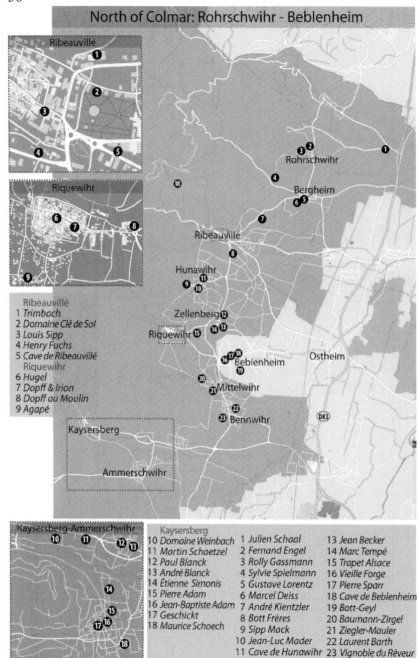

Ribeauvillé
1 Trimbach
2 Domaine Clé de Sol
3 Louis Sipp
4 Henry Fuchs
5 Cave de Ribeauvillé
Riquewihr
6 Hugel
7 Dopff & Irion
8 Dopff au Moulin
9 Agapé

Kaysersberg
10 Domaine Weinbach
11 Martin Schaetzel
12 Paul Blanck
13 André Blanck
14 Étienne Simonis
15 Pierre Adam
16 Jean-Baptiste Adam
17 Geschickt
18 Maurice Schoech

Kaysersberg
1 Julien Schaal
2 Fernand Engel
3 Rolly Gassmann
4 Sylvie Spielmann
5 Gustave Lorentz
6 Marcel Deiss
7 André Kientzler
8 Bott Frères
9 Sipp Mack
10 Jean-Luc Mader
11 Cave de Hunawihr
12 Edmond Rentz

13 Jean Becker
14 Marc Tempé
15 Trapet Alsace
16 Vieille Forge
17 Pierre Sparr
18 Cave de Beblenheim
19 Bott-Geyl
20 Baumann-Zirgel
21 Ziegler-Mauler
22 Laurent Barth
23 Vignoble du Rêveur

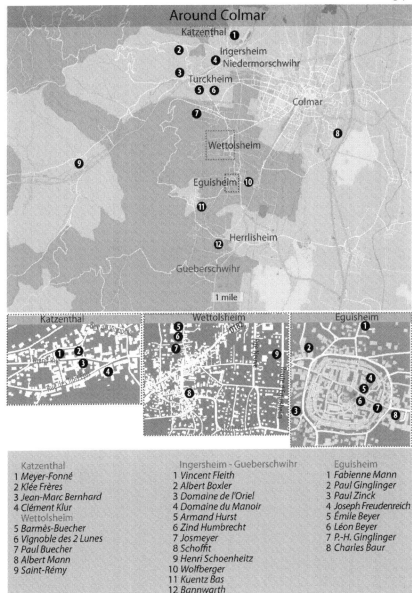

Katzenthal
1 Meyer-Fonné
2 Klée Frères
3 Jean-Marc Bernhard
4 Clément Klur
Wettolsheim
5 Barmès-Buecher
6 Vignoble des 2 Lunes
7 Paul Buecher
8 Albert Mann
9 Saint-Rémy

Ingersheim - Gueberschwihr
1 Vincent Fleith
2 Albert Boxler
3 Domaine de l'Oriel
4 Domaine du Manoir
5 Armand Hurst
6 Zind Humbrecht
7 Josmeyer
8 Schoffit
9 Henri Schoenheitz
10 Wolfberger
11 Kuentz Bas
12 Bannwarth

Eguisheim
1 Fabienne Mann
2 Paul Ginglinger
3 Paul Zinck
4 Joseph Freudenreich
5 Émile Beyer
6 Léon Beyer
7 P.-H. Ginglinger
8 Charles Baur

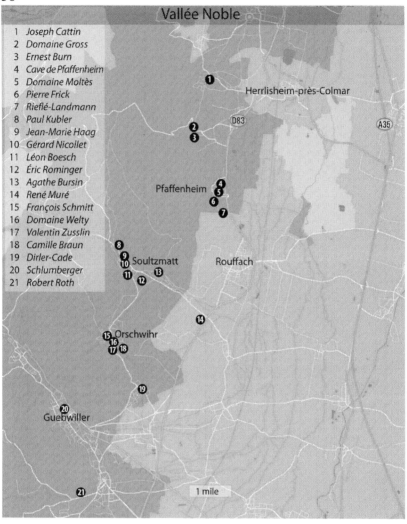

Vallée Noble

1 Joseph Cattin
2 Domaine Gross
3 Ernest Burn
4 Cave de Pfaffenheim
5 Domaine Moltès
6 Pierre Frick
7 Rieflé-Landmann
8 Paul Kubler
9 Jean-Marie Haag
10 Gérard Nicollet
11 Léon Boesch
12 Éric Rominger
13 Agathe Bursin
14 René Muré
15 François Schmitt
16 Domaine Welty
17 Valentin Zusslin
18 Camille Braun
19 Dirler-Cadé
20 Schlumberger
21 Robert Roth

Herrlisheim-près-Colmar

D83

A35

Pfaffenheim

Soultzmatt

Rouffach

Orschwihr

Guebwiller

1 mile

Profiles of Leading Estates

Ratings	
***	Excellent producers defining the very best of the appellation
**	Top producers whose wines typify the appellation
*	Very good producers making wines of character that rarely disappoint

Symbols	

Address

Phone

Owner/winemaker/contact

@ Email

Website

Red   White   Sweet
Reference wines

Grower-producer

Negociant (or purchases grapes)

Cooperative

Conventional viticulture

Sustainable viticulture

Organic

Biodynamic

ha=estate vineyards

bottles=annual production

Tasting room with especially warm welcome

Tastings/visits possible

By appointment only

No visits

Sales directly at producer

No direct sales

Winery with restaurant

Winery with accommodation

Domaine Agapé　*

10, rue des Tuileries,
68340 Riquewihr

+33 3 89 47 94 23

Vincent Sipp

domaine@alsace-agape.fr

www.alsace-agape.fr

Riesling, Schoenenbourg

Vendange Tardive, Alsace Riesling

10 ha; 65,000 bottles
[map p. 36]

"I come from the Sipp family of Ribeauvillé; my grandfather and his brother founded Louis Sipp. I worked in Hunawihr for fifteen years with my brother, then I created this small winery ten years ago. I wanted to have my own winery, to be smaller and have my own style," says Vincent Sipp. Located on the outskirts of Riquewihr, the winery is a workmanlike building with a tasting room at the front. Vineyards are one third grand cru. Almost all the rest are on middle slopes, mostly in (potential) premier crus. The vineyards in Riquewihr were purchased, others in Ribeauvillé and Hunawihr are rented.

Wines are divided into three ranges. "The idea is to separate dry wines from the sweet or semi-sweet. Sweetness is a big problem for Alsace," Vincent explains. The Expression range consists of blends from the middle slopes. Then there are the grand crus, mostly vinified dry. Helios is used to describe sweet or semi-sweet wines. Aging for whites is typically 70% stainless steel, 20% in foudres, and 10% in barriques. Reds are aged only in barriques.

The Riesling style is relatively restrained, even for the Expression cuvée. There are Rieslings from three grand crus. Rosacker is the most mineral and backward, Osterberg is quite reserved but tends to spicy herbal impressions, and Schoenenbourg is the softest and most approachable. The style is dry or very close to it. The Pinot Blanc is actually 100% Auxerrois. "In cold years I put Auxerrois on the label because the mineral character is more pronounced," Vincent says. Pinot Gris is in the fruity spectrum, but even from the grand crus it is labeled Sec (although it is not quite bone dry). Gewürztraminer from Schoenenbourg has less sweetness than the variety usually displays, bringing out typicity. Vendange Tardive cuvées of Riesling, Pinot Gris, and Gewürztraminer all maintain freshness, with Riesling showing a characteristic piercing purity (partly explained by its origins as a blend from grand crus Rosacker and Osterberg). "We only make Vendange Tardive when it's really good," Vincent says. In fact, the Vendange Tardive may reach the standard for SGN.

Domaine Barmès-Buecher   *

30 rue Sainte Gertrude,
68920 Wettolsheim

+33 3 89 80 62 92

Sophie Barmès

@ info@barmes-
buecher.com

www.barmes-
buecher.com

Riesling, Steingrubler

Gewürztraminer,
Rosenberg

17 ha; 100,000 bottles
[map p. 37]

"I am the third generation, both sides of my family were vignerons," says Genevieve Barmès. The domain was founded by merging two domains after Genevieve (Buecher) married François Barmès. François was a driving force for a move to quality, moving to biodynamic viticulture in 1998, and bottling his own wines instead of selling grapes. Sadly François died in an accident in 2011, and the domain is now run by Genevieve together with her children, Maxim (the winemaker) and Sophie (marketing).

Vineyards are mostly around Wettolsheim, with some in neighboring villages, and include three grand crus. The most important lieu-dit is Rosenberg, close to Wettolsheim. There are 15-20 cuvées, depending on whether late harvest wines are made, and whether all the grand crus are made. Élevage depends on vintage, but usually the Rieslings are kept in stainless steel, and the various Pinots in demi-muids or foudres. Wines are divided into dry, which here is regarded as less than 6 g residual sugar, and Vin d'Esprit Sec (wines in dry style) between 7 g and 15 g.

Blended from Chardonnay, Auxerrois, and Pinot Blanc, the Crémant is always vintage and zero dosage. "It is dry but not acid, and I would say that the Pinot family is more important than the Chardonnay," Genevieve says. Zero dosage follows the general policy of no additives for all wines.

Pinot Noir is planted on limestone terroirs, always at high density on hillsides. The Reserve Cuvée is a blend from several parcels. The Vieilles Vignes comes for 50-year-old-vines on the grand cru Hengst. Grapes are sorted and destemmed, there is punch-down during fermentation, and then maturation in barriques, with the Reserve spending 12 months and the Vieilles Vignes taking 16 months (and including some new oak). The minerality of the Reserve intensifies on the Vieilles Vignes.

Rieslings are an exercise in terroirs. Rosenberg is the softest, Clos Sand is more mineral, grand cru Steingrubler is elegant, and Hengst is powerful. Pinot Gris tends to a mineral style; the Rosenberg cuvée is dry unless the year is very warm. Gewürztraminers are really elegant, from the delicacy of Rosenberg (coming from the top of the hill which is windy, ensuring freshness) to the power of Hengst. Although they are sweet, the general impression of the style is drier than the residual sugar would suggest; they are subtle expressions of the variety in which typicity is not muddied by sweetness.

Domaine Léon Beyer ★★★

8 place Château St Léon (shop)

2 Rue de La 1ere Armée, 68420 Eguisheim

+33 3 89 21 62 30

Marc Beyer

contact@leonbeyer.fr

www.leonbeyer.fr

Riesling, Les Ecaillers

20 ha; 450,000 bottles

[map p. 37]

This is one of the most traditional houses in Alsace—"Viticulteurs de Père en Fils depuis 1580"—formally founded in 1867. Vineyards, including an additional 40 ha that the Beyers work but do not own, are in the vicinity of Eguisheim. All of Alsace's varieties are represented, although Sylvaner is not being replanted. Beyer takes pride in making wines to accompany food, which means that everything is vinified bone dry (except for Vendange Tardive or SGN). "Typical and classic Alsace wines are, and always have been, dry, fresh and light."

Vinification is in very old foudres, and the wine spends eight months on the lees, but vintages are often released somewhat later than other producers. Marc Beyer says that, "The style of the house has not changed in the past fifty years, except that yields have decreased so concentration has increased."

The dry wines fall into three ranges: Classic, Reserves, and Grandes Cuvées. As Marc Beyer is one of the strongest critics of the grand cru system, Beyer's own names are used for the Grandes Cuvées, although the Riesling Les Ecaillers comes from the grand cru Pfersigberg, and the Riesling R de Beyer is from grand cru Eichberg. The top wines carry the label Comte d'Eguisheim, and are made only in the best years. They include Pinot Gris and Gewürztraminer, as well as Riesling, again from grand cru vineyards. They age well: the Riesling 2000 was vibrant and lively in 2014. Beyer also produces several Eaux de Vies.

There's a tasting room in the center of Eguisheim, although wines are made at a facility just outside the town.

Domaine Paul Blanck ★★

32 Grand-Rue, 68240
Kientzheim, Alsace

+33 3 89 78 23 56

Philippe Blanck

info@blanck.com

www.blanck.com

Furstentum, Pinot Gris

Furstentum, Riesling

32 ha; 160,000 bottles
[map p. 36]

"My grandfather Paul established the domain in the 1920s, but we are the nineteenth generation of growers in the village, although there's nothing special about that," says Philippe Blanck, who runs the domain today with his cousin Frédéric, the winemaker. Vineyards are local: "The idea is to work the vineyards around the valley of Kaysersberg, it's interesting because we have many different types of soil here," Philippe explains. The range of dry wines is divided between the Classic Cuvées and Vins de Terroir. About 60% of production, the Classic Cuvées include all the varietals, and are vinified dry, or almost dry, in stainless steel, and bottled under screwcap. The Vins de Terroir come from lieu-dits or grand crus. After fermentation in stainless steel, they mature for twelve months in foudres. Here the natural richness is expressed by allowing some residual sugar. "The people who buy the Vins de Terroir know the wines so they aren't confused by varying sweetness," Philippe says. The style tends generally to richness, even at the Classic level, where there is often a buttery undercurrent. The range includes an impressive array of seven grand crus, with six in Riesling, and three each in Pinot Gris or Gewürztraminer. Riesling varies from the delicacy of Furstentum to the richness of Wineck-Schlossberg, and the sheer grip of Sommerberg. Pinot Gris and Gewürztraminer show great character, often with a lovely savory or herbal counterpoise to the typical sweetness.

Domaine Léon Boesch   *

6 rue Saint Blaise,
68250 Westhalten

☎ +33 3 89 47 66 16

Mathieu Boesch

@ boesch@domaine-boesch.fr

⊕ www.domaine-boesch.fr

🍶 Gewürztraminer, Les Fous

🍶 Riesling, Breitenberg

🍷 Vendange Tardive, Zinnkoepflé Gewürztraminer

😊 🎩 🍇 🌓

14 ha; 90,000 bottles
[map p. 38]

ALSACE
APPELLATION ALSACE CONTRÔLÉE

"Les Fous"
GEWURZTRAMINER
Domaine Léon Boesch
GÉRARD ET MATHIEU BOESCH PROPRIÉTAIRES SOULTZMATT ET WESTHALTEN FRANCE

The Boesch family has been located in Soultzmatt since 1640, and they moved to their present location, on the road between Soultzmatt and Westhalten, right under the grand cru of Zinnkoepflé, a mere 150 years ago. Mathieu Boesch and his wife Marie represent the eleventh generation. The charming house that serves as a tasting room and offices was built by Mathieu's parents, and Mathieu built a new cellar in 2010.

The new cellar typifies the domain's approach. Made of local materials, it feels as though it has been there a very long time. "We were looking to make the building a bit like we make the wine, traditional and new at the same time," Mathieu says. "We wanted to make a cellar with the ambience of an old cave. We constructed it in stone because for us the cellar is the continuation of the terroir." Only the barrels are really old. "Old wood means more than ten years; we don't want to have a taste of wood." Everything is vinified in wood, using old foudres for the whites, and barriques for the reds.

All the vineyards are within a kilometer of the winery. Local conditions suit the house style. "We are in a valley here with cool nights. The deeper you go in the valley, the cooler it gets. We harvest early to keep freshness. With organic and biodynamic viticulture, we don't need to go to 13% alcohol to get ripeness, so we get ripeness at much lower alcohol." The driving force is to keep the wines fresh, whether they are red or white. "The Pinot Blanc, La Cabane, comes from a vineyard near the forest and we like that because it keeps freshness. Pinot Blanc from the plain can be too fat." It's a turnaround and sign of global warming that Mathieu prefers cooler sites for Riesling and Pinot Noir. "We haven't made grand cru Riesling since 2013—we used to have Zinnkoepflé—which could be good in cool vintages, but hot vintages lose character."

All the wines are dry, except for two cuvées each of Pinot Gris and Gewürztraminer that are doux (semi-sweet) or late harvest. Is it difficult to get Pinot Gris dry? "Not for me—but some vignerons would be afraid of not getting ripeness." The consequence of the dry style, helped by picking early, is that varietals show their essential character without being muddied by sugar. Pinot Blanc shows stone fruits, Pinot Gris is a little spicy, Pinot Noir has red berry aromatics, Muscat has restrained grapey perfume, Riesling is taut with citrus impressions, Gewürztraminer shows its usual perfumed spectrum but is unusually elegant. Cool vintages suit the style here better than warm.

The Gewürztraminers are especially good, increasing in intensity from the Alsace AOP, Les Fous, to grand cru Zinnkoepflé, but always subtle and retaining acidity due to unusual conditions of the valley. "Here in the valley there's a lot of Gewürztraminer, it really likes the climate of hot days but not too hot, and cold nights," Mathieu explains.

There is a rare sense of delicacy to the sweet Gewürztraminers, which include vin doux (from the communal area Vallée Noble) and Vendange Tardive (from Zinnkoepflé). Mathieu stopped making the SGN after 2012 because he believes the Vendange Tardive has a better balance. All the wines, even the late harvest, show that fresh character that epitomizes the house style.

Domaine Bott-Geyl ★★

⚲ *1 rue du Petit Château,*
68980 Beblenheim

📞 *+33 3 89 47 90 04*

📠 *Jean-Christophe Bott &*
Valérie Bott-Geyl

@ *info@bott-geyl.com*

⊕ *www.bott-geyl.com*

▎ *Riesling, Grafenreben*

[symbols]

22 ha; 85,000 bottles
[map p. 36]

Located in a back street of Beblenheim, surrounded by suburban housing, the building is much larger than it appears from the outside, as a new three storey warehouse-like gravity-feed winery was constructed three years ago on top of the old caves. Vinification is in a mix of stainless steel and old foudres; most cuvées have some of each. The key to the style here is that fermentation is very slow, lasting several months, so the wines are bottled in the summer following the vintage, as by then there has been ample extraction.

Jean-Christophe Bott doesn't have a set idea about style: "Each vintage imprints its character," he says. Although he tries to pick early, he believes the balance may differ with the vintage, so the wines are not necessarily dry. Jean-Christophe's aim of producing dry wines is usually achieved with Riesling, but balance in Pinot Gris and Gewürztraminer generally requires some residual sugar.

The wines are divided into Vins d'Assemblage (blends of varieties), Vins de Fruits (Les Eléments: Riesling, Muscat, Pinot Gris, and Gewürztraminer), and the Vins de Terroir (which includes lieu-dits and no less than six grand crus); and then of course the sweet wines. By the time you reach the vins de terroir, most of the wines do in fact have a touch of residual sugar. The style here often has a delicious sweet-sour balance, with savory impressions counterpoised with the fruits. It's always measured, so that Pinot Gris and Gewürztraminer show their character without overwhelming.

Domaine Albert Boxler ★★

78 Rue Trois Epis, 68230
Niedermorschwihr

+33 3 89 27 11 07

Jean Boxler

@ albert.boxler@9online.fr

Riesling, Brand

14 ha; 60,000 bottles
[map p. 37]

Discretely located in the main street of the town (no sign is evident in the street, but when you go round the back, the winery and the family house are organized around a charming courtyard in typical Alsace style), the domain is just under the grand cru of Sommerberg. This is very much a family domain; I tasted with Jean Boxler in the house, with children playing in the next room. Boxlers have been here since the seventeenth century, but the domain was created by Albert Boxler in 1946 when he started to bottle his own wine. His grandson Jean has been making the wine since 1996.

Most of the 30 individual vineyard parcels are in the immediate neighborhood, including several that are used to make different cuvées from Sommerberg. All of the cépages are grown here, but the focus is on Riesling, which is 40% of plantings. Everything is vinified as whole cluster, and there's a tendency to vinify the sweet wines in stainless steel and the dry wines in oak, but it doesn't always exactly work out.

The Riesling is usually dry, but the Pinot Gris is usually demi-sec. Jean is not a fanatic about dryness and believes that the overall balance is more important. A pleasing sense of restraint characterizes all Albert Boxler's wines. Contrasting with the natural acidity there is a common warm softness. A consistent style runs across cépages, intensifying in Riesling, and then from Alsace to Grand Cru to Vieilles Vignes Grand Cru. Even the Crémant shows precision.

48

Domaine Marcel Deiss

**

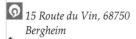

15 Route du Vin, 68750
Bergheim

+33 3 89 73 63 37

Matthieu Deiss

marceldiss@marceldeiss.fr

www.marceldeiss.com

Riesling, Rotenberg

32 ha; 150,000 bottles
[map p. 36]

My last discussion with Jean-Michel Deiss had a surreal air. I found him doing the pigeage, physically immersed in a cuve of Pinot Noir, in the old way. I had to perch on top of a ladder leaning against the vat to talk with the disembodied head of Jean-Michel as he wallowed in the must. Jean-Michel has the air of a fanatic. "Cépage is a nonsense, it's a modern concept. It's impossible to make a great wine from a single cépage," he says.

But he is a fanatic for making wine true to what he sees as the ancient tradition of Alsace: from more than one variety rather than from a single cépage. He is quick to point out that he does not produce his wines by assemblage, the mixing of wines made from different varieties, but each wine is produced from grapes of different varieties that are inter-mingled (complanté) in the vineyard. Indeed, floating in the must of the Pinot Noir were several bunches of white grapes.

Production here offers both conventional and unconventional wines. The wines are grouped as Vins de Fruits (the usual varieties of Alsace, vinified as single varietals); Vins de Terroirs (wines from specific vineyards, including grand crus: whites consist of various varieties intermingled, and reds consist of Pinot Noir with small amounts of other varieties); and Vins de Temps, which are late harvest wines.

Mathieu has also introduced an alternative label, Vignoble du Rêveur (see mini-profile), which he uses for wines from new vineyards he has acquired. Among the four wines, Singulier is an unusual carbonic maceration of a blend of Riesling and Pinots, and the most recent cuvée is an orange wine, Un Instant sur Terre, made from Gewürztraminer and Pinot Gris.

Domaine Dirler-Cadé ✱

13 Rue Issenheim, 68500 Bergholtz

📞 +33 3 89 76 91 00

👤 Ludivine Dirler

@ dirler.cade@orange.fr

🌐 dirler-cade.com

🍾 Gewürztraminer, Saering

🍾 Pinot Gris, Bux

🍾 Vendange Tardive, Kessler Gewürztraminer

☺ 🏭 🍇 🍷

18 ha; 80,000 bottles

[map p. 38]

ALSACE GRAND CRU
Saering
APPELLATION ALSACE GRAND CRU CONTROLEE
DIRLER-CADÉ
Vendanges Tardives
Riesling
2011
Mis en bouteille à la propriété par
DIRLER-CADE EARL VITICULTEURS À 68500 BERGHOLTZ - FRANCE
PRODUIT DE FRANCE

This is very much a family business. In the tasting room at the weekend, Ludivine Dirler was busy with a group of cavistes, her daughter was manning the counter for a group of tourists, her father-in-law was tasting with a journalist, and her granddaughter was playing. The winery is organized around a courtyard in the main street of Bergholtz, and the spacious tasting room on one side has an extensive selection of cuvées. With roughly 25 cuvées, even for Alsace this is an unusually broad range, and many are available in more than one vintage. It's a very good experience for the tourist.

The domain was created four generations ago in 1871 by Jean Dirler. The name of the domain and its present form dates from the marriage in 2000 between Jean Dirler (great grandson of the first Jean Dirler) and Ludivine Hell-Cadé, when Domaine Hell-Cadé joined with Domaine Dirler. Soils are quite varied, with sandstone, calcareous terroir, some clay, and some volcanic plots. Grapes are pressed as whole clusters, and then vinification is traditional, using a mix of foudres and stainless steel. The vineyards have been biodynamic since 1998.

There are three ranges of wines. Alsace AOP for each variety is the entry-level, the lieu-dits are intermediate, and there are four grand crus. "The grand crus have always been separate, but we only started to make the lieu-dits separately more recently," says Ludivine Dirler. All the vineyards are around Bergholtz and the neighboring town of Guebwiller, essentially within 300 m to 3 km of the winery. About half of the vineyards are grand cru.

The style of the Rieslings is understated, and they tend to be quite closed for first three or so years. They extend from Alsace AOP, to lieu-dit Belzbrunnen (near grand cru Siegel), to four grand crus, with Kitterlé and Kessler quite tight, but Saering somewhat broader. The Alsace Riesling is dry, but Belzbrunnen and the grand crus usually have a just-detectable touch of residual sugar. Saering and the cuvée H.W. from a plot in the center of Kessler have the greatest potential to age.

All the Muscats come from grand crus. They are a mix of Muscat Ottonel and Muscat d'Alsace. Because of global warming the Muscat d'Alsace is ripening better, so is a greater proportion than before. They are vinified dry. Pinot Gris is usually off-dry with a characteristic spectrum of stone fruits.

Gewürztraminer is the standout here, with all four grand crus represented, and offering the greatest complexity of any of the varieties. The restraint of Saering showcases the character of the grape, Kitterlé tends to be sweeter and more obvious, the ripeness of Kessler can approach Vendange Tardive in style in warm years, and the Kessler Vendange Tardive balances the nature of the variety against botrytis.

Domaine Rolly Gassmann **

📍 *15 Grande Rue, 68580 Rorschwihr*

📞 *+33 3 89 73 33 06*

👤 *Pierre Gassmann*

@ *rollygassmann@wanadoo.fr*

🍾 *Riesling, Silberberg*

🍾 *Pinot Gris, Rotleibel*

🍾 *Gewürztraminer, Rorschwihr*

☺ ⚒ 🍇 🍷

52 ha; 300,000 bottles

[map p. 36]

Rolly Gassmann's tasting room was opposite the church in the small square that is the center of Rorschwihr. Basically it was a corner of a large warehouse used for stockage. But a huge new facility has been constructed up the street next to the old winery (which dates from 1976). In addition to a modern winery, there's a tasting room overlooking the vineyards, "and maybe a restaurant, who knows?" says Pierre Gassmann as he shows you around. "It's a regrouping rather than an expansion," he explains. At all events, the modern winery built into the hillside is quite a contrast with the old houses of the village.

Pierre is a very energetic fellow. This is very much a family business as all three generations of the family were busy in the tasting room, which is always open, and has an extensive list of wines. Pierre's policy is to release wines when they are ready—or at least when they are approachable—and this requires a lot of stockage; the cave contains about four vintages' worth of wines. The list of wines in the tasting room include older vintages back to 1989.

Rolly and Gassmann are two old names in the village, and the domain comes from the marriage of Marie-Thérèse Rolly and Louis Gassmann in 1967; Pierre is their son. With vineyards in three villages, this is a relatively large domain for Alsace. There are no grand crus, but many different cuvées from individual plots or selections. "We keep each plot different as the geology is different—we have 35 different soil types," Pierre says.

The domain is controversial for its style. "We want to have grapes as ripe as possible with as much minerality as possible. We usually harvest about two weeks after everyone else, and harvest lasts about 18 days. Our philosophy is to make wines that age. It's not the acidity that supports aging, it's the physiology and maturity of the plant" The result is that the wines usually have a touch of botrytis and some residual sugar. "The policy of dryness does not exist here. They are sweet but they are in balance and will age long term. After 8-10 years the wine usually eats the sugar and tastes drier."

The wines are characterful. Later harvest really pays off for Sylvaner and Auxerrois, where the contrast between botrytis versus herbal or mineral notes gives a lift to the palate. Even the Sylvaner has some life, and the Auxerrois ("we've always separated Auxerrois and Pinot Blanc") is quite lively. Pinot Gris is quite savory, often showing a balance between its characteristic mushrooms and the sweetness of botrytis. Gewürztraminer is generally spicy, with the characteristic roses and lychees pushed into the background, making a subtle impression with more finesse than the variety usually displays. Sometimes the concentration results in a touch of bitterness at the end. The Pinot Noirs mature quite early.

That same contrast between herbal and sometimes floral notes against the background of sweetness reinforced by botrytis shows for Riesling, where it is accentuated by impressions of steely minerality. Everything is flavorful, with minerality contrasting with the sweetness and sometimes dominating it. Even the Vendange Tardive and SGN cuvées maintain that herbal impression to offset against the sweetness. Vendange Tardive cuvées do not taste as sweet as would be expected from the numbers, so there is less difference than elsewhere compared with the regular cuvées. All along the line, the wines are distinctive and flavorful, but you have to accept some sweetness and a touch of honey.

Domaine Paul Ginglinger ★

◎ *8 Place Charles de Gaulle,*
68420 Eguisheim

📞 *+33 3 89 41 44 25*

👤 *Michel Ginglinger*

@ *info@paul-ginglinger.fr*

🌐 *www.paul-ginglinger.fr*

🍶 *Pinot Gris, Eichberg*

🍶 *Riesling, Eichberg*

😊 🏭 🍇 🧹

12 ha; 80,000 bottles
[map p. 37]

Michel Ginglinger is the twelfth generation at this family domain, where he's been in charge since 2000. "We have been involved with wine since the sixteenth century," he says, "we are deeply focused on the terroir." Just out of the center of Eguisheim, the family house is on one side of a courtyard, which extends back from the road with practical-looking winery buildings around. Michel's father is manning the busy tasting room at the front.

Virtually all the vineyards are around Eguisheim, comprising about 50 parcels, including the grand crus Eichberg and Pfersigberg. There are 19 cuvées, but, "This is not so big for an Alsatian estate, we try to keep it simple," Michel says, explaining that outside of the grand crus, there is one cuvée for each grape variety. "Everything is dry, except the Gewürztraminer, of course. And the Pinot Gris is not dry analytically, but is in the spirit of the dry wine. We want always to have a good minerality in the wine. It needs to be dry to clearly express terroir." In Pfersigberg, two different plots are distinguished for Riesling: Ortel is more mineral, Hertacker is broader.

The entry-level wines are attractive and delicate. Grand crus have more intensity but retain the generally clear and delicate style. Even though Pinot Gris has a touch of residual sugar, it's barely obvious, and the sweetness in the Gewürztraminer integrates well. Ginglinger's best wines come from the Eichberg grand cru. The Riesling is broad, reflecting the clay-calcareous soils, but still has racy minerality and lots of flavor, and the Pinot Gris shows the powerful character of Eichberg.

Famille Hugel **

📍 *3 Rue de La 1ère Armée, 68340 Riquewihr*

📞 *+33 3 89 47 92 15*

👤 *Marc Hugel*

@ *info@hugel.com*

🌐 *www.hugel.com*

🍷 *Pinot Noir, Les Neveux (Jubilee)*

🥂 *Riesling, Jubilee*

☺ 🏭 🍇 🍾 🍃

30 ha; 1,200,000 bottles

[map p. 36]

Maison Hugel dates from the seventeenth century and is run by Marc and his cousin Jean-Philippe (the twelfth generation since the house was founded in 1639; Marc's brother Étienne sadly died young in 2016). The winery occupies a picturesque rabbit warren of buildings in the old town of Riquewihr. The tasting room is always open and always busy. Hugel is one of the larger negociant-growers, with estate vineyards providing about a quarter of its grapes. Half of the estate vineyards are organic, the other half are managed by lutte raisonnée; grapes are purchased from another 100 ha.

There are five lines of wines. Classic is the entry-level (from purchased grapes). Tradition is the mid range (based on stricter selection of purchased grapes). Jubilee was used for the top cuvées, coming only from estate vineyards, but was replaced in 2010 by a new range, Grossi Laüe (Alsace dialect for great growth), which comes from specific sites, grand crus Schoenenbourg (Riesling) and Sporen (Gewürztraminer), and lieu-dit Pflostig (Pinot Gris and Pinot Noir). Like Jubilee, it is always dry.

The dry style is something Étienne felt strongly about: "It's a very serious problem that affects the whole image of Alsace, with wines being made in sweet styles." Only the late harvest wines, Vendange Tardive and SGN, are sweet. "At Hugel we have only two categories: dry and sweet. We are different from most producers where most wines are in the middle," says Marc. Are there problems getting Pinot Gris and Gewürztraminer to dryness? "It's tricky, you need to assemble from different terroirs. If a grower has only one parcel on a grand cru, he doesn't have any option."

Hugel produces all of the Alsatian varieties, and was a pioneer in introducing Pinot Noir as a serious red wine. One Pinot Noir originated when a half hectare vineyard of Pinot Noir planted in 1966 came up for sale in 1985. The Hugel family refused to buy it, so Étienne and Marc and a cousin (the three nephews) bought it. Johnny Hugel wanted to uproot it and replant with a white variety! It's now the heart of the Jubilee Pinot Noir; sometimes there is a separate cuvée which they call Les Neveux.

Hugel are well known for their rejection of the grand cru system—"The grand cru classification is meaningless as an indication of quality"—so their wines are labeled only as Alsace, although Marc admits, "More than half of our vineyards are in grand crus, and in the best parcels at that, so it's absolutely surreal not to have grand cru on the label." The Grossi Laüe Riesling from Schoenenbourg, and the Gewürztraminer from Sporen, are in fact the defining wines for these grand crus. The introduction of a new Riesling cuvée, called Schoelhammer after a climat in Schoenenbourg, may indicate some softening in position; this is intended to be the top cuvée of Riesling.

Domaine Josmeyer ★★

🎯 *76 Rue Clémenceau,*
68920 Wintzenheim

📞 *+33 3 89 27 91 90*

👤 *Céline Meyer*

@ *info@josmeyer.com*

🌐 *www.josmeyer.com*

🍷 *Riesling, Les Pierrets*

☺ ♕ 🍇 ◖

25 ha; 160,000 bottles
[map p. 37]

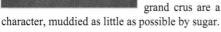

"We make dry white wines to go with food," says Céline Meyer, who runs Domaine Josmeyer together with her sister Isabelle. Created in 1854 by Alois Meyer and transferred down the generations, the domain is located in charming buildings around a courtyard in typical Alsace style, on the main street. Vineyards are mostly local, but spread out over many small parcels, about 80 in all. Vinification is traditional, with everything matured in old foudres.

The focus here is classic: after a quick excursion into Pinot Blanc and Auxerrois (including the Pinot Auxerrois "K" cuvée which comes exclusively from old Auxerrois vines), tasting focuses on Riesling, Pinot Gris, and Gewürztraminer. Going up the range of Rieslings, flavors turn from petrol (in Le Kottabe from the plain) to citrus (in Les Pierrets from the slopes) to stone fruits (in grand crus Brand and Hengst), and the wines become increasingly reserved. In spite of the commitment to dry style, alcohol levels are moderate.

These are not wines for instant gratification, but need time for full flavor variety to emerge. The top wines are the Rieslings from Brandt and Hengst. They do not really come out of their shell in the first five years. Then Brand rounds up beautifully, while Hengst is more austere and needs longer; if you can use the term in Alsace, it is a vin de garde. A similar transition is seen with Pinot Gris, from the classic Fromenteau (Alsace AOP) to Brand and then Hengst: these are as dry as Pinot Gris gets, increasing in richness and power along the range. For Gewürztraminer, Les Folastries is almost dry, and the grand crus are a bit richer. The style brings out varietal character, muddied as little as possible by sugar.

Domaine Marc Kreydenweiss ★★

12, rue Deharbe, 67140 Andlau

+33 3 88 08 95 83

Antoine Kreydenweiss

marc@kreydenweiss.com

www.kreydenweiss.com

Riesling, Wiebelsberg

14 ha; 70,000 bottles

[map p. 35]

Located towards the northern tip of the Alsace vineyards, the Kreydenweiss domain was established in the seventeenth century, has been bottling wines since the mid nineteenth century, and includes vineyards that belonged to the Abbaye of Andlau before the French Revolution. The tasting room is located in a charming old house in the village.

Marc Kreydenweiss has been running the domain since he took over in 1971 at the age of 23. He was one of the first in Alsace to adopt biodynamic viticulture, and in 1984 decided to focus on single-vineyard wines; most of the dozen cuvées come from named plots, culminating in three grand crus.

The Kreydenweiss operation has expanded beyond Alsace, first by purchasing the Perrières domain near Nîmes in 1999, and then by extending a negociant activity to Châteauneuf-du-Pape. In fact, more wine is now made in the south than at the original estate in Andlau.

In Alsace there are also brandies made from Riesling, Pinot Gris, and Gewürztraminer, as well as eux-de-vie Mirabelle. An unusual feature of vinification here is that malolactic fermentation is encouraged, but this does not seem to detract from the freshness of the wines. The grand cru Rieslings have a penetrating minerality, and the lieu-dit wines follow the same style with less intensity. Pinot Gris often has savory overtones to balance the residual sweetness. Purity is the mark of the house, enhanced by low yields (around 40 hl/ha).

Domaine Paul Kubler   *

103, 68570 rue de la
Vallée, Soultzmatt

+33 3 89 47 00 75

Philippe Kubler

contact@paulkubler.com

www.paulkubler.com

Gewürztraminer,
Zinnkoepflé

9 ha; 50,000 bottles
[map p. 38]

Philippe Kubler is the third generation of winemakers in the domain, which was established in 1947, although winemaking in the family goes back to the seventeenth century. The wines are divided into three ranges. The entry-level "K" series is AOP Alsace. The "vins de terroir" come from lieu-dits or grand crus and are dry (off-dry for Gewürztraminer). The "liquoreux" are sweet, either Vendange Tardive or SGN.

The "K" Riesling comes from younger vines, and the steely, mineral impressions intensify with the Breitenberg cuvée, which comes from a site at the far west, cool because it is close to the Vosges.

Pinot Gris varies in sweetness with the vintage, but Philippe's heart is with the dry style. "People have an idea that Pinot Gris is demi-sec but I want to make wine that is more Burgundian in style than Alsatian," he says, perhaps reflecting his time working in Burgundy. The "K" Pinot Gris tends to savory; grand cru Zinnkoepflé, from a cool plot at the very top of the hill, intensifies that impression almost to the point of umami in vintages where it is dry.

Gewürztraminer shows the classic character of roses and lychees, just off-dry in the "K" cuvée, and more intense from Zinnkoepflé. "In Zinnkoepflé there will never be heavy sweetness, it always stays very fine and fresh, this is the essence of Zinnkoepflé."

When Philippe introduces the cuvée La Petite Tête au Soleil, he explains that the name is the French translation of "Zinnkoepflé." "This is our flagship wine," he says, explaining that the variety is not mentioned on the label, because it is Sylvaner and people react adversely to the name of the varietal. "We are one of the last producers making Sylvaner on Zinnkoepflé, but Zinnkoepflé used to be famous for Sylvaner; before the AOC was created, it was 25% of plantings." Coming from 70-year-old vines, La Petite Tête au Soleil is a rare example of Sylvaner that shows the character of the variety. All the wines here are characterful, with a tendency to move in a savory direction.

Domaine Albert Mann ***

📍 *13 rue du Château, 68920 Wettolsheim*

📞 *+33 3 89 80 62 00*

✉ *Marie-Claire or Marie-Thérèse Barthelmé*

@ *vins@albertmann.com*

🌐 *www.albertmann.com*

🍷 *Pinot Noir, Clos de la Faille*

🍶 *Riesling, Furstentum*

🍶 *Pinot Gris, Cuvée Albert*

😊 🏛 🍇 ⬭

23 ha; 120,000 bottles
[map p. 37]

The Mann and Barthelmé families have been making wine in Wettolsheim since the seventeenth century. "Albert Mann was my father in law," says Maurice Barthelmé. "He was one of the first to start bottling his own wine, 1947. When I arrived, I worked with him making the wine, while my brother was involved with the Barthelmé family estate. When my father died in 1989 we joined the two domains. Now my brother makes the wine and I mostly look after the vineyards."

Divided into almost a hundred different plots, the vineyards include five grand crus that represent about a third of the total. There are about 25 cuvées, including all the varieties except Sylvaner, which was taken out a few years ago. Entry-level wines have been bottled under screwcap since 2004; now all the whites except the grand crus are under screwcap. The domain is known for its hands-off approach. "We don't do oenology or make technical wine," says Maurice. "Our philosophy is to capture the terroir. We work with stainless steel tanks for the white wines, because we want to preserve the purity of the fruits, and it lets us work with less sulfur. Reds are handled like Burgundy." Tastings are held at the old domain headquarters in Wettolsheim, but winemaking was moved to a new cellar outside the village in 1991.

There's an unusual emphasis on Pinot Noir, with no less than four single vineyard cuvées: Clos de la Faille (a monopole close to Hengst) and Les Saintes Claires from lieu-dits, and Grand P and Grand H from the Pfersigberg and Hengst grand crus. Tasting here starts with reds. "You have to taste some reds to see how in one house you can produce complex Pinot Noirs. We have a high reputation for Pinot Noir, we have some old parcels of Pinot Noir." The vines came from a selection of pre-phylloxera vines from the Mosel. Tasting the range is like going from the Côte de Beaune to the Côte de Nuits. Clos de la Faille is lively, Les Saintes Claires is more structured, Grand P is elegant and feminine (my favorite for its elegance), while Grand H is muscular and masculine. They are well up to the standard of premier crus in Burgundy.

The entry-level line (called Traditions) is fruity and approachable, and mostly off-dry. Cuvée Albert describes blends of Riesling or Pinot Gris from parcels that are not in grand crus. The style here is always complex. Rieslings from the lieu-dits and grand crus are steely or broad, depending on terroir, and vary from dry to overtly sweet; Cuvée Albert has a subtle balance of citrus fruits with petrol, Schlossberg is steely, and Furstentum is the opposite, all steely. They age beautifully, indeed they require it. "Our Rieslings need 5-6 years to be ready to drink," says Maurice. "The Rieslings are dry, but not like you find in Burgundy, we are not prophets of dryness. When a wine finds its balance, we don't want to change it." In a tasting at the domain going back to the nineties, the older Rieslings and Pinot Gris were coming into their own. Pinot Gris is off-dry or sweet; "Pinot Gris is harvested ripe, it's not quite dry, but it goes in a dry direction. It is never dry because when it's ripe we always have a little sweetness." Gewürztraminer is always sweet. "I like a little botrytis in the grand crus because it increases complexity," Maurice says, but the mark of the subtlety of the house is that the sweetness always seems much less than the numbers would suggest.

Maurice summarizes his philosophy: "Some negociants have a style, in a vertical it is easier to see the house style than the vintage, but for our wines each vintage is distinct."

Domaine Jean-Louis & Fabienne Mann   *

*11, Rue du Traminer,
68420 Eguisheim*

+33 3 89 24 26 47

Sébastien Mann

contact@vins-mann.com

www.vins-mann.com

*Riesling, Alsace Vieilles
Vignes*

Pinot Gris, Rosenberg

*13 ha; 50,000 bottles
[map p. 37]*

Brimming over with enthusiasm, Sébastien Mann says, "The domain is very modern—my parents are very modern." Sébastien joined his parents Jean-Louis and Fabienne in the domain in 2009, and persuaded his father to move from organic to biodynamic viticulture ("Papa didn't believe in it at first, but it was a revelation"). Sébastien believes that 90% of the work is in the vineyard, where harvest is decided by tasting the pips. "We collect whole bunches, and we don't have a sorting table, I want the harvesters to know how to select the raisins we want."

Except for Pinot Noir and Muscat, everything is pressed as whole bunches. Influenced by a period in Champagne, Sébastien introduced a second pneumatic press in order to be able to press everything very gently and slowly. "Pressing is the key thing in vinification. We press very gently to get the heart of the juice. Then there is a small settling and I've finished my work."

Sébastien's grandfather actually bottled his own wine until 1945, but after that sent grapes to the cooperative. (The domain had 5 ha and was known as Henri Mann.) Jean-Louis took over in 1982, and the modern history of the domain started in 1998, when Jean-Louis resumed bottling. The domain is located in an old house in Eguisheim, with caves underneath, and a small tasting room located separately just around the corner. Vineyards come from both sides of the family, roughly half in Eguisheim (from Jean-Louis) and half in Ingersheim (from Fabienne). Everything is vinified by parcel, and almost all the whites are handled in stainless steel. "It's magnificent for optimizing the fruits." There are many cuvées. "There are few domains of this size that have 35 cuvées," Sébastien comments.

Wines are divided into four ranges. All of the Alsace Terroirs are absolutely dry (with less than 1g of residual sugar), except for the Gewürztraminer. Cuvée Fabienne et Jean-Louis comes from riper grapes and has a little residual sugar. The grand crus are usually dry, except for the Gewürztraminer and sometimes the Pinot Gris. And then of course there are the late harvest wines.

The Rieslings point in the direction of herbs and minerality, from the Alsace Vieilles Vignes, which comes from 60-75-year-old vines ("this is my most gourmand Riesling"), to the tight Logelberg ("this needs 10-15 years"), the salinity of lieu-dit Altengarten, and the two cuvées of Pfersigberg. Pfersigberg consists of two hills, and there is a block on each; the first is labeled Pfersigberg alone, and is faintly perfumed and herbal, while the second is labeled as #2, and is more intense and savory.

The dry Pinot Gris cuvées need two or three years for flavors to emerge, but then convey a savory impression. Rosenberg epitomizes the house style, poised between savory and fruity. Letzenberg is an exception that is made like Burgundy in old barriques. "We are known for our dry Pinot Gris," Sébastien comments, "but if you want dry Pinot Gris, you have to be very careful about harvest; in two days it can get botrytis and go up three degrees. My father made Rosenberg sweet, but I make it dry." The Eichberg grand cru Pinot Gris is sweet, however.

The style is thoughtful, adjusting to the terroir. Sébastien recalls his experience with the Eichberg Pinot Gris. "We bought the parcel in 2011. The first year I vinified it as sweet, the second as dry, I had to understand the parcel. Now it's liquoreux again, I think it's very good terroir for dry, but great for liquoreux."

Meyer-Fonné Vins   **

24 Grand'rue, 68230 Katzenthal

+33 3 89 27 16 50

Felix Meyer

felix@meyer-fonne.com

www.meyer-fonne.com

Riesling, Pfoeller

14.5 ha; 85,000 bottles

[map p. 37]

With a spectacular view from his living room window of the fortress on top of the hill of the Wineck-Schlossberg grand cru, Felix Meyer is right under the vineyards. The Meyer family have been in Katzenthal since 1732; Felix's great grandfather created the domain. The family house is at one end of the courtyard; at the other end are the winery buildings, where everything has been modernized. Felix has been in charge since 1992. He expanded the estate from an initial 6 ha, and now there are vineyards all around the local area, including several grand crus. Riesling and Pinot Blanc are the most important, but all the varieties are made except Sylvaner. There are usually 22-30 cuvées depending on whether there is VT and SGN.

The focus is on terroir. "I'm very interested in terroir and passionate about it, we work on five grand crus and three lieu-dits, and this goes back twenty years so it's not something new," Felix says. The first level of wines, Alsace AOP and some Katzenthal village cuvées, are always vinified to dryness, and bottled in the Spring to preserve freshness. The lieu-dits and grand crus usually have a minimal touch of residual sugar, and are bottled just before the next harvest. Felix tries to be consistent. "Each cuvée has a single style, I don't want a cuvée to be sweet one year and dry another year," he says. The Rieslings are quite textured at lower levels and have a tendency to power at the grand cru level. Pinot Gris and Gewürztraminer tend to be quite forceful.

Domaine René Muré ★★

📍 Clos Saint Landelin, Route du Vin, RN 83, 68250 Rouffach

📞 +33 3 89 78 58 01

👤 Véronique Muré

@ domaine@mure.com

🌐 www.mure.com

🍷 Pinot Noir, V (Vorbourg)

🍷 Riesling, Clos St. Landelin

😊 🏭 🍇 🍶 🍽

25 ha; 150,000 bottles
[map p. 38]

This family domain has been producing wine since the seventeenth century. Véronique and Thomas Muré, the twelfth generation, work with their father René. In addition to estate vineyards, they buy grapes from growers under long term contract for around another 30 ha. The winery is just south of Rouffach, overlooked by grand cru Vorbourg, which includes the Clos St. Landelin, a lieu-dit at the southern tip that is a monopole purchased by René Muré in 1935. Wines are divided into those under the René Muré label, and those under the Clos St. Landelin label, which include grand crus around Rouffach.

Vinification is in old foudres (some more than a century old, but with internal temperature control). The wines spend 15 months on the lees. There are all the varieties, with a full range from dry to vendange tardive and SGN, but the Rieslings and Pinot Noirs are the signature wines here. Pinot Noir has increased in proportion with the recent run of warm vintages (a return to the past as Rouffach was known for red wines in the Middle Ages). "Clos St. Landelin, it's paradise for Pinot Noir," says René. "Fifteen years ago we only had 10%, now it's more like 15-20%."

The Murés are concerned about the effects of global warming in increasing alcohol levels, and have been experimenting with Syrah. "My father was forced to harvest the Pinot Noir very early with a series of hot vintages," says Thomas Muré, "so we tried some other varieties." A small experimental plot of Syrah gave its first commercial yield in 2015, and one barrel has been bottled as a Vin de France. It shows a pure style following the Northern Rhône, and the Murés are waiting to see if it gains complexity as the vines age. "The Syrah has 12.5% alcohol, the Pinot Noir has 13.5%, so this is good for returning to the old dates of harvest," Thomas says.

Wines under the René Muré label are intended for consumption relatively soon, but those under the St. Landelin label should have longevity of one to two decades. Riesling is intense and racy. The style is completely dry. "We look to have dry wines, really dry, less than 2 g sugar," Thomas says. Clos St. Landelin is the flagship, where the focus is on freshness and minerality; it is a textbook example of dry Riesling from Alsace. "Riesling is planted on the lower slopes where it gets the wind, so it is fresher than the top where we plant Pinot Noir and Gewürztraminer." Pinot Noir is very fine, showing an earthy character with impressions of minerality. "In the red wines are looking to express the terroir, not to make wines that show off tannins and extraction."

Domaine Ostertag ★★

📍 *87 rue Finkwiller, 67680 Epfig, Alsace*

📞 *+33 3 88 85 51 34*

📇 *André Ostertag*

@ *info@domaine-ostertag.fr*

🌐 *domaine-ostertag.fr*

🍇 *Pinot Gris, Muenchberg*

15 ha; 90,000 bottles

[map p. 35]

This domain was created by André's father in 1966, but he abruptly handed over the winemaking in 1980 to André when he was only twenty. There's more freedom to innovate here than in a domain bound by a long history. Behind the unassuming front on a back street in Epfig is a charming courtyard, surrounded by winery buildings. André essentially works the domain alone, using only estate grapes from his 75 individual vineyard plots. "This is crucial because the major part of quality comes from the work in the vineyards," André says.

There are three series of wines: the basic series are AOP Alsace, there are some grand crus, and then there are the Vendange Tardive or SGNs. Except for the latter and for the Gewürztraminer, all the wines are dry. The Pinot Blanc is matured in barrique and (unusually for Alsace) goes through malolactic fermentation. In fact, the grand crus are sometimes refused the *agrément* on grounds of lack of typicity (because of exposure to new oak), and a compromise has been reached in which the name of the grand cru is put on the back label rather than stated on the front.

About 7-8% of production is Pinot Noir, which also is matured in barriques rather than the traditional foudres. There is 100% destemming to make the wine as soft as possible, and délestage (a procedure in which the must is racked off and pumped back) is used rather than punch-down. The village wine uses one third oak and is bottled in July.

Domaine André & Lucas Rieffel   *

11 Rue Principale, 67140 Mittelbergheim

+33 3 88 08 95 48

Lucas Rieffel

andre.rieffel@wanadoo.fr

Riesling, Brandluff

Pinot Gris, Kirchberg de Barr, La Colline aux Escargots

Vendange Tardive, Wiebelsberg Riesling

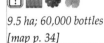

9.5 ha; 60,000 bottles

[map p. 34]

– Rieffel –

GRAND CRU
WIEBELSBERG

RIESLING

LUCAS ET ANDRE RIEFFEL VIGNERONS

"My grandfather started bottling just after the second world war, the first bottling was actually a Sylvaner. My father expanded the estate from its initial 1.6 ha to its present size by buying vineyards," says Lucas Rieffel, who took over in 1996. "10 ha is enough for the moment. I'm planning to replant rather than expand, I want to improve the quality first."

What has changed since Lucas took over? "Everything! The first thing to change was the yields. I think they are too high in Alsace. We are moving to organic viticulture. We've changed to slower pressing and longer élevage in the cellar, and we don't use sulfur except for bottling. Each year we work more in the vineyard and less in the cellar." A policy of noninterference extends to MLF: unusually for Alsace, usually it happens.

"Except for Gewürztraminer, we want to make all the wines dry, but sometimes it's difficult. I prefer to make the wine with good balance even if there is some residual sugar rather than to make it dry just to say it's dry. It depends on the vintage." It's a sign of the modern approach that screwcaps have been used since 2008 for everything except Pinot Noir and grand crus. "But we've done one grand cru this year, maybe soon it will be everything. If the market accepts it, I would like to use screwcaps for everything."

Picking starts with the Crémant, and then continues directly for everything else, "so usually we pick early." The style of whites is dry. "The intention is to drink in one to three years, we feel that wines retain their fruitiness best for the first three years." For my palate, the wines seem relatively closed on release, then as they open up, showing as zesty and lively with restrained fruit flavors. Fruits come out after a couple of years, perhaps three years for the grand crus, and they become more mineral after five years.

Rieslings are aged in stainless steel on total lees; Pinot Blanc and Pinot Gris age in old barriques. The Rieslings here really begin to be expressive after three years. Wiebelsberg from sandstone is more floral, Brandluff with more clay is quite closed on release but really shows minerality after five years, Zotzenberg is rounded and spicier and more generous. Pinot Gris has that interesting blend of fruity and savory impressions, the Gebreit cuvée of Pinot Blanc comes from Pinot Blanc and Auxerrois in complantation on granite and is quite lively ("my father used to make a Crémant, but we thought it was beautiful and would make a still wine"), and there are several Sylvaners culminating in grand cru Zotzenberg (the only grand cru where Sylvaner can be produced). The Pinot Noirs show a modern take on old Alsace; bright, but generally light in character.

Domaine Martin Schaetzel ✱

◎ *15C Route du Vin,*
68240 Kientzheim

📞 *+33 3 89 47 11 39*

Marc Rinaldi

@ *contact@martin-*
schaetzel.com

🌐 *www.martin-*
schaetzel.fr

🗑️ 🏭 🌰 🗂️

13 ha; 45,000 bottles
[map p. 36]

This is effectively that rare thing, a new domain in Alsace. The background is a little unusual. Martin Schaetzel was a well regarded small producer in Ammerschwihr for the past 80 years. When Jean Schaetzel retired in 2015 (he is now a consultant), Marc Rinaldi bought the brand and the stock. A major attraction was the vineyard holdings on granitic terroirs, half in grand cru Brand and half in Schlossberg. Marc loves Riesling from granite: "I prefer Riesling from granite, it's more straight," he says. "I bought vineyards in Schlossberg and Brand because they are on granite."

A stylish new winery has been constructed on the main road into Kaysersberg, just opposite Schlossberg, with a large sign on the front saying "Schaetzel by Kirrenbourg" (Kirrenbourg is a lieu-dit in Schlossberg). The very smart building is crammed with equipment, stainless steel tanks for vinification, and barriques for aging the reds, with a tasting room at the front.

Brand and Schlossberg represent most of the vineyards, with a little more in Hengst and some Pinot Noir elsewhere. Brand and Schlossberg represent most of the vineyards, with a little more in Hengst. Estate grapes account for 80% of production, and the vineyards are converting to biodynamics. Purchased grapes come from organic vineyards, and are the basis for the Cuvée Reserve line (which is being phased out). The focus will be on estate vineyards as the domain gets into its stride. "In the future we will have three levels of wine. The top level is grand cru. The second level is Terroir, called "S." The third level will be "Granite," representing wines all from the same terroir, e.g. Schlossberg." The basic idea is that each lot will be classified into one of these levels. "We have four locations for Riesling in Schlossberg and they are all vinified separately. We taste in the summer, then we decide what level each should be. This method of thinking is more Bordeaux than Alsace. Other domains don't like to do different wines from a grand cru, they like to call it all grand cru, but I don't understand that, for me grand cru should be the best," Marc explains.

Is there a policy about residual sugar? "Dry, dry, dry! But when you get a year like 2015 you do get a little sugar from the vintage," Marc explains. The Rieslings tend to a savory style, increasing in intensity until reaching the peak in Schlossberg. Indeed, Schlossberg is the peak for all the major varieties, Pinot Gris as well as Gewürztraminer. Pinot Gris is not so common on granitic soil, but the Schlossberg cuvée has a very fine texture with a flavor spectrum poised between fruity and savory in an off-dry style in a warm vintage. Schlossberg Gewürztraminer shows a classic spectrum of roses and lychees, but with great refinement. Pinot Noir comes from limestone terroir close to Schlossberg and is in a lighter style. This is presently a small domain, but worth watching for developments.

Domaine Schlumberger   *

📍 *3 rue des Cours Popu-
laires, 68500 Guebwiller*

📞 *+33 3 89 74 27 00*

👤 *Séverine Schlumberger*

@ *mail@domaines-
schlumberger.com*

🌐 *www.domaines-
schlumberger.com*

🍷 *Pinot Gris, Kitterlé*

🍷 *Riesling, Kitterlé*

😊 🏭 🍇 🍷

130 ha; 650,000 bottles

[map p. 38]

Schlumberger's vineyards are in a long contiguous block running along the hillside (really more like a mountain slope) parallel with the town of Guebwiller, which nestles under the mountain. Vineyards are mostly at elevations of 250-350 m. To visit the vineyards, Séverine Schlumberger drives you up from the town in a Landrover. As the road goes up from the town, it narrows into little more than a muddy path running along a ledge between successive terraces of vineyards, with a sheer drop to the vineyards below. At one point it becomes so narrow that you are asked to get out and walk ahead while the car inches along behind, rather than risk everyone in the Landrover. It's around this point, Sevérine says with a wicked grin, that they usually ask clients if they'd like to complete the order form.

Established with Nicolas Schlumberger's purchase of 20 ha in 1810, today Schlumberger is one of the larger landholders in Alsace, with half of the holdings in the four grand crus around Guebwiller. "We don't believe in following fashions, which come and go, but make very much the same mix of varieties and styles as traditionally," Séverine says. Vinification is in foudres of very old oak. The wines are divided into Les Princes Abbés (with all seven of the varieties), the Grand Crus (with Riesling, Pinot Gris, and Gewürztraminer), and Les Collections (Vendange Tardive or SGN dessert wines). All wines come exclusively from the estate, and are very reliable.

Domaine François Schmitt   *

19 Route de Soultzmatt,
68500 Orschwihr

+33 3 89 76 95 33

Myriam Schmitt

info@francoisschmitt.fr

www.francoisschmitt.fr

Gewürztraminer, Bollen-berg

Riesling, Bollenberg

Vendange Tardive, Al-sace Riesling

13 ha; 110,000 bottles
[map p. 38]

"It's an old family, but a new business," says Myriam Schmitt. "The family has been involved in wine since 1697, but was selling the grapes until my father-in-law started bottling in the 1970s. Frédéric took over in 1997." The domain is on the main road through Orschwihr, in quite a large modern-looking building, with a new tasting room. Vineyards are around the village, with most in the lieu-dit Bollenberg or the grand cru Pfingstberg; half belong to the domain, half are rented from members of the family.

There are three ranges of wines. AOP Alsace is for entry-level wines, sometimes coming from purchased grapes (but harvested by the domain). The next level up comes from estate holdings in lieu-dit Bollenberg (you can see it from the door of the tasting room, with vineyards facing west). The Le Maréchal cuvée of Pinot Gris comes from a single plots in Bollenberg and the Marie-France cuvée of Gewürztraminer is a selection of the best lots from Bollenberg. The top wines come from grand cru Pfingstberg, which is across the road from Bollenberg, facing east.

Vinification is in stainless steel, except for the top cuvées of the Pinots, which mature in barriques, with a little new wood. The style is committed to dryness. "We try to vinify everything to dryness, except for the Pinot Gris and Gewürztraminer. We like acidity in the wine, we like the wine to be gastronomic." The Bollenberg cuvées tend to be slightly spicy. The style carries through to the Pfingstberg Riesling, and then the Paradis cuvée, from a plot which has limestone as well as sandstone, shows more austerity. The Pinot Gris and Gewürztraminer are fine examples of the dry style, with the Gewürztraminer increasing in intensity, and becoming more savory, moving from Bollenberg to Marie-France and then to Pfingstberg.

Domaine Schoffit   *

66-68 Nonnenholzweg par Rue-des-Aubepines, 68000 Colmar

+33 3 89 24 41 14

Alexandre Schoffit

domaine.schofit@free.fr

Riesling, Rangen Clos St. Théobald

16 ha; 120,000 bottles

[map p. 37]

The domain has an obscure location at the end of a tiny road through a housing estate close to the autoroute on the eastern edge of Colmar, yet there is a constant stream of visitors to the tasting room. Vineyards extend from Colmar to the south. The most important are in grand cru Rangen (well to the south at the end of the grand crus), where 25 years ago Bernard Schoffit bought 6.5 ha around Clos St. Théobald that had been considered too steep to work. Now fully planted, this is the heart of the domain.

There are all the cépages of Alsace, with a majority of Riesling. Depending on the year, there are 20-30 cuvées. Fermentation is allowed to proceed until it stops naturally, which usually leaves a little residual sugar for Riesling and Pinot Blanc, 12 g/l for Pinot Gris, and 30 g/l for Gewürztraminer. In the introductory range (Tradition), the wines taste drier than in the Caroline range, which is richer. Cuvée Alexandre is used for wines that are sweet but not labeled as Vendange Tardive.

There's a steady increase in complexity from AOP Alsace to lieu-dit Harth to grand cru. Sommerberg (only available in small amounts for old clients) increases in complexity; the top of the range is Rangen and the wines from the Clos St. Théobald monopole within it. For Riesling, Sommerberg showcases tense acidity and Rangen brings out delicacy. The Gewürztraminers are unusually subtle at levels ranging from sweet through VT to SGN. Vendange Tardive for both Pinot Gris and Gewürztraminer shows its character more as texture and flavor variety than overt sweetness; lovely if you want the flavor spectrum without too much sweetness.

Domaine Sipp Mack

📍 *1 Rue Vosges, 68150 Hunawihr*

📞 *+33 3 89 73 61 88*

👤 *Laura Sipp*

@ *contact@sippmack.com*

🌐 *www.sippmack.com*

🍷 *Riesling, Alsace Tradition*

🍷 *Gewürztraminer, Alsace Vieilles Vignes*

🍷 *Pinot Gris, Rosacker*

😊 🏭 🍇 🚜

24 ha; 150,000 bottles

[map p. 36]

The domain was formed in 1959 when François Sipp of Ribeauvillé married Marie Louise Mack of Hunawihr. Each had about 6 ha of vineyards, and since then the size of the state has been doubled by purchases. Almost all the vineyards are on calcareous-clay soils. The winery is in Hunawihr, close to grand cru Rosacker, which is the most important holding. A large yellow building on the street has the tasting room and offers accommodation: the rooms are used for pickers during harvest. The domain has been run by Jacques Sipp and his wife Laura since 1983, now with their daughter Caroline.

The approach is traditional, with the nature of the wines depending on the vintage. "We like always to be under 5 g residual sugar, but sometimes it's not possible. When fermentation sticks at 6 g, adding more yeast would be a shame because you would lose the flavor," Jacques explains. Everything is handled in stainless steel except for Pinot Noir and Pinot Blanc. "I think we have more precision in white wine making when we use stainless steel."

Tradition is the entry-level line. "We feel that Tradition should be very good because it's our calling card," is Jacques' view. The Riesling is dry and quite mineral, Pinot Gris is off-dry but tastes less sweet than the level of residual sugar suggests, Gewürztraminer is off-dry and quite perfumed. Coming from a blend of plots in four potential premier crus, the Riesling Vieilles Vignes shows more intensity; the Gewürztraminer Vieilles Vignes is beautifully integrated.

There's an interesting comparison for both Pinot Gris and Riesling between the Osterberg and Rosacker grand crus. Pinot Gris from Osterberg is sweeter. "Originally we wanted to make Osterberg as dry Pinot Gris, but we couldn't, so we decided to go with what nature gives us, and that naturally comes to 25 g residual sugar," Jacques says. Rosacker Pinot Gris is more inclined to a savory direction, with a complex blend of stone fruits, mushroom, and spices.

Rosacker Riesling is held back for release until about five years after the vintage. It's quite backward, with steely minerality, and usually dry. It comes from two blocks in Rosacker: one at the extreme western end is very dry and high with yellow calcareous stone; a smaller block is lower down and near Clos Sainte Hune. Osterberg Riesling is always rounder and more forward.

The general impression here is mainstream, with each variety allowed to express itself without being forced into a pattern.

Maison Louis Sipp ★★

⊙ 5 Grand'rue, 68150
  Ribeauvillé

📞 +33 3 89 73 60 01

👤 Etienne Sipp

@ louis@sipp.com

🌐 www.sipp.com

🍷 Riesling, Osterberg

⚠️ 🏭 🍇 🛢️ 🏺

40 ha; 200,000 bottles

[map p. 36]

In charge of this family domain since 1996, Etienne Sipp has a thoughtful, quasi-academic approach, perhaps explained by his Ph.D. in mineral science. Created after the first world war, the domain has been located right in the center of picturesque Ribeauvillé since 1933. Today production comes exclusively from estate grapes, "From the historical part of the vineyards on the slopes," Etienne says. "Our vineyards are concentrated in a radius of 3-4 km," he adds, explaining that this is an area within a fractal field that is exceptionally diverse in its soil types. "Geology and climate are very specific here, which is why we can produce a high diversity of wines. The only negative is that the wines do not open quickly; they age well but need some time to open."

Under a yellow label, the entry-level range is divided into young wines and Nature'S wines, the latter being organic; the Reserve Personelle wines have longer aging before release. There are five single vineyards and two grand crus in the cuvées from specific terroirs, as well, of course, as late harvest. Purity of style allows vintage influence to show directly, as illustrated by a vertical of Riesling from Osterberg: 2010 is steely citrus, austere and needing time; 2009 is soft pleasure, with a smile of sweetness on the stewed citrus; 2008 is all delicate citrus; 2007 is more reserved; 2004 is quite floral. Pinot Gris and Gewürztraminer are more forward, and here the reserved style can translate into delicacy.

Maison Pierre Sparr & Fils

10 rue de Hoen, 68980 Beblenheim

+33 3 89 78 24 22

Corinne Perez

info@vins-sparr.com

www.vins-sparr.com

130 ha; 800,000 bottles
[map p. 36]

This old negociant has a complicated history that led to decline. It was divided between two brothers, each had two sons, and in 2007 there was a split; one side of the family left, the rest remained. (There's still a Sparr making wines but he isn't allowed to use the name.) The negociant went into bankruptcy and was bought by the cooperative at Beblenheim in 2009.

Today Sparr owns 15 ha and buys grapes from 240 ha. Some of the growers are very small, so there are some cuvées from amalgamating lots from several grand crus based on commonality of terroir. There is no distinction on the label between estate and purchased grapes. The scale of production is large: "too many to count," is the answer when you ask how many cuvées there are. Headquarters is a rather commercial looking establishment in Sigolsheim.

Grand Reserve is the entry-level wine. It's under cork for France and Belgium, screwcaps elsewhere. Vincent Lallier came as winemaker in 2007 to modernize production, focus more on fruit, protect against oxidation, and use longer élevage on the lees. It's fair to say that there are real efforts at improving quality, but you have to go to the grand cru level to see it. The best wine to my mind is the atypically austere Mambourg grand cru Riesling. Grand cru Altenbourg or the terroir-based Alsace Sol Granitique are more typical, with discernible residual sugar.

Domaine Marc Tempé ★★

24 rue de Schlossberg,
68340 Zellenberg

+33 3 89 47 85 22

Marc Tempé

@ marctempe@wanadoo.fr

⊕ www.marctempe.fr

Riesling, Grafenreben

8 ha; 40,000 bottles
[map p. 36]

Located in an old house in the square in Zellenberg, the domain looks like it might go back eons, but in fact was started by Anne-Marie and Marc Tempé in 1993 when they obtained vineyards from their parents, who were retiring as members of the cooperative. "We asked ourselves what we should do with 7 ha, we had a clean slate, we weren't obliged to follow the history of our parents and grandparents. It was obvious to me that I should make wine as I wanted," says Marc. The domain remains small and hands-on: Marc came back from the vineyards on his tractor for our tasting.

The clean slate has led to a distinctive style in which the wines have long élevage in barriques. "My aim is to make a dry wine because it goes best with food. Fermentation is never stopped here because the wine stays two years in cave with no intervention. It will find an equilibrium even if sometimes there is residual sugar," explains Marc. So some of the wines have a minimal level of sugar, just at the level of detection, but perfectly integrated.

The wines are flavorful, with Rieslings generally soft but delicate, yet conveying a definite sense of silky texture. Pinot Gris shows its character with a herbal texture, and Gewürztraminer conveys an unusual sense of varietal character without becoming overwhelming. The Vendange Tardive or SGN Gewürztraminer is a knockout for its delicacy. In fact, if a single word describes the domain it's that delicacy of character running through the range.

Maison Trimbach **

15 Route de Bergheim,
68150 Ribeauvillé, Alsace

+33 3 89 73 60 30

Pierre Trimbach

contact@trimbach.fr

www.trimbach.fr

Riesling, Frédéric Emile

60 ha; 1,000,000 bottles
[map p. 36]

One of the most important houses in Alsace, Trimbach remains a hands-on family business. "I can still drive a fork lift when needed," says Pierre Trimbach. The winery on the main road through Ribeauvillé has a quaint appearance—Trimbach goes back to 1626—but wine production is entirely modern. Trimbach owns enough vineyards to supply about a third of its grapes. Estate vineyards are organic; purchased grapes come from growers who practice lutte raisonnée.

Trimbach's heart is in Riesling, which is more than half of production. Riesling is always completely dry, and Pinot Gris and Gewürztraminer are vinified as dry as balance will allow. The basic Riesling is 30-35% of production. The Riesling Reserve comes 95% from estate vineyards in the local vicinity, with 50-year-old vines. The vineyards are picked separately for this cuvée and worked like the grand cru. The Selection de Vieilles Vignes is a selection within the Reserve category, made for the first time in 2009, and since then when there has been enough crop.

The Trimbachs do not believe in the grand cru system, although the wines for their top Rieslings come from grand cru terroir. Cuvée Frédéric Emile comes from the vineyards immediately behind the winery, which run across two grand crus, Geisberg and Osterberg. Osterberg is always more upright, Geisberg is always richer. There are 6 ha, but not all the plots are used in every vintage. Clos St Hune comes from 1.67 ha in grand cru Rosacker.

"The vines in Frédéric Emile and Clos Sainte Hune have similar ages, they give the same yields: the difference is the terroir." Recently, Trimbach have in fact introduced the first grand cru, a Geisberg Riesling (which is distinctly richer in style than Frédéric Emile); the Geisberg vineyard has been rented from some nuns, who insisted that the name of the grand cru should appear on the label.

Yellow labels identify the Classic and Réserve lines. Gold labels indicate the terroir wines, which include Frédéric Emile Riesling, Réserve Personelle Pinot Gris, and Seigneurs de Ribeaupierre Gewürztraminer; these come only from estate grapes. White labels are the very peak, including Clos Sainte Hune and the Vendange Tardive and SGN. The style of Riesling is mineral, saline, bordering on austerity; going up the hierarchy, increasing time is needed for development, a couple of years for Réserve, five years for Geisberg, eight for Frédéric Emile, and at least a dozen for Clos Sainte Hune, which is widely acknowledged as one of the top Rieslings of Alsace.

The hierarchy can be quite deceptive here. Going from the entry-level appellation to the Reserve and then to the Vieilles Vignes selection from the Reserve, there is greater refinement, but less overt fruits, more restraint and minerality, and more time is needed to open. Going to Frédéric Emile and Clos Sainte Hune, flavor is less apparent on release, it needs time to come out. So in a horizontal tasting of a young vintage, you don't see the increase in quality in an overt expression of fruits, you have to look beyond that to get an impression of future potential. And we may be talking about many years here. The top cuvées are wines for the ages.

Domaine Weinbach ***

25 Route du Vin, 68240
Kaysersberg

+33 3 89 47 13 21

Catherine Faller

contact@domaineweinbach.com

www.domaineweinbach.com

Riesling, Cuvée Colette

Pinot Gris, Cuvée Sainte
Catherine

30 ha; 120,000 bottles
[map p. 36]

There always seems to be a zany scene when I visit Domaine Weinbach. On one occasion, there were constant changeovers in who conducted the tasting as people juggled their responsibilities, on another the pickers were having lunch in the kitchen and we tasted around them, most recently there were simultaneous tastings taking place in the kitchen, the dining room, and elsewhere. But in spite of the superficial appearance that everything is happening at once, this matriarchal domain makes some of the most precise and elegant wines in Alsace. With holdings in four grand crus as well as the Clos des Capucins and other lieu-dits, there are many cuvées.

It really doesn't matter if the variety is Riesling, Gewürztraminer or Pinot Noir: there is always that precise delineation of flavors. The name on the label says Domaine Weinbach, but the wall surrounding the Clos de Capucines at the heart of the vineyard (across the road from the hill of grand cru Schlossberg) says Domaine Faller on one side and Le Weinbach (the name of the lieu-dit) on the other. The domain was acquired in 1898 by the Faller brothers, inherited by Théo Faller, and after 1979 run by his wife, Colette, and her daughters Catherine and Laurence. 2014 was a sad year for the domain because Laurence, the talented young winemaker, died unexpectedly in May, followed later by Colette. Catherine and her family continue, with her son Théo now the winemaker.

All the varieties are produced, and the wines are vinified dry with some notable exceptions. Gewürztraminer is usually off-dry and Pinot Gris sometimes has a little residual sugar. Where else do you find such elegant Muscat or refined Gewürztraminer, let alone the granular Pinot Gris, poised between fruity and savory, and the steely Rieslings? The style here is not at all the usual nondescript quality for Sylvaner or simple grapey notes for Muscat. Sylvaner, Pinot Blanc, Muscat all tend towards a more savory impression than usually expressed by these varieties, with faint overlay of richness for Sylvaner, a savory/fruity balance for Pinot Blanc, and a fine granular, savory impression for Muscat. Domaine Weinbach's fame lies with the great white varieties, but that wonderfully precise style of the domain comes through to the "W" Pinot Noir, silky, smooth, and elegant.

The Rieslings are certainly the top of the line. Coming from old vines in the middle of the Clos des Capucines, Cuvée Théo highlights the style of the house for Riesling: smooth and silky, with a precise, steely impression of minerality supported by racy acidity. With Cuvée Colette, which comes from 45-year-old vines on the lower slopes just going into Schlossberg, you begin to see the style of the grand cru: a little rounder, then smooth and silky, with great depth. The Schlossberg cuvée *tout court* comes from 50-year-old vines at the top of the hill and shows restrained depth. Coming from the oldest (65-year) parcels in the middle of the slope of Schlossberg, Cuvée Catherine shows the intensity of the full force grand cru experience. Sainte Catherine l'Inédit, which comes from the best parcels in Schlossberg in the best years, is an exception that often has a touch of residual sugar.

Domaine Zind Humbrecht ***

📍 *4 Route de Colmar, 68230 Turckheim*

📞 *+33 3 89 27 02 05*

👤 *Olivier Humbrecht*

@ *contact@zind-humbrecht.fr*

🌐 *www.zindhumbrecht.fr*

🍾 *Riesling, Herrenweg de Turckheim*

40 ha; 200,000 bottles
[map p. 37]

Created in 1959 with the marriage of Léonard Humbrecht to Geneviève Zind, this domain has become one of the best regarded in Alsace under the leadership of their son Olivier, who took over in 1989. Humbrechts have been making wine here since the seventeenth century. The domain moved to a stylish new building in the Herrenberg vineyard in 1992. Zind-Humbrecht was a pioneer in bio-dynamic viticulture and in reducing yields, typically now around 30-40 hl/ha. One consequence is increased rich-ness, which is allowed to show itself by levels of residual sugar that vary with the vintage; the domain was one of the first (in 2001) to indicate the level of sweetness by marking it on the label against a five point scale.

Most wines are bottled as lieu-dits, so there are around 30 cuvées altogether. The best known are perhaps Clos Windsbuhl (close to the Rosacker grand cru) and Clos Saint Urbain (a monopole within the Rangen grand cru). The only generic wines are Zind (a Chardonnay-Auxerrois blend from Windsbuhl labeled as Vin de France), Pinot Blanc, Riesling, and Muscat. The Calcaire cuvées come from calcareous terroirs. Then there are 7 Rieslings from lieu-dits or grand crus, 4 Pinot Gris, and 4 Gewürztraminers as well as the vendange tardive and SGN. The hands-off approach makes it hard to find a single description for the style, but it tends to a rich and powerful expression of each variety. Olivier has been skeptical about Pinot Noir in Alsace, so the emphasis remains on whites, but in 2009 he produced a Pinot Noir from a plot of vines planted at high density on limestone terroir at Heimbourg.

Domaine Valentin Zusslin ***

🎯 *57 Grand'rue, 68500 Orschwihr*

📞 *+33 3 89 76 82 84*

📇 *Marie & Jean Paul Zusslin*

@ *info@zusslin.com*

🌐 *www.zusslin.com*

🍷 *Pinot Noir, Bollenberg Harmonie*

🥂 *Riesling, Clos Liebenberg*

😊 🏭 🍇 🍸

16 ha; 90,000 bottles

[map p. 38]

Jean-Paul and his sister Marie are the thirteenth generation to run this family domain since the Zusslins moved from Switzerland three centuries ago to settle in Orschwihr, where there are now several producers called Zusslin in the Grand'Rue. Their history is emphasized by a huge genealogical chart of the Zusslins on the wall of the tasting room.

Riesling is the most important variety, but unusually Pinot Noir is close behind. The main three cuvées are the Rieslings from Bollenberg (a lieu-dit), Clos Liebenberg (a monopole close to grand cru Pfingstberg), and Pfingstberg. Rieslings are pressed slowly for 10-12 hours, settled, and fermented in foudres. The style is racy, a very pure and precise expression of the variety, with intensity and savory overtones increasing from Bollenberg to Clos Liebenberg to Pfingstberg. A vertical of Pfingstberg similarly shows savory elements increasing with age and beginning to turn tertiary after ten years.

The Bollenberg Harmonie Pinot Noir (Harmonie is the best plot for reds in Bollenberg) offers smooth red fruits supported by silky tannins and lovely aromatics. It's de-stemmed, vinified in wooden cuves, and matured in barriques with 50% new oak. The impression is softer and more aromatic than Burgundy, but very fine. About five years after the vintage is the right time to start the reds.

In some years there is a vendange tardive Riesling from Pfingstberg, which is extraordinarily subtle; in fact, subtle is the one word that sums up the domain.

Mini-Profiles of Important Estates

Jean-Baptiste Adam

5 Rue Aigle, 68770 Ammerschwihr

+33 3 89 78 23 21

Laure Adam

jbadam@jb-adam.fr

www.jb-adam.com

20 ha; 800,000 bottles

[map p. 36]

This venerable house, which functions as both domain and negociant, celebrated 400 years in Ammerschwihr in 2014. After taking over in 1996, Jean-Baptiste V, modernized and expanded the winery. In 2005, he purchased Kuentz-Bas (see mini-profile). Laure Adam is now taking over from her father, with her husband Emmanuel Boyer as winemaker. The domain is well-known for its Kaefferkopf, as it is one of relatively few growers to produce this grand cru, from which it makes several cuvées of Riesling, Gewürztraminer, or blends. The Vieilles Vignes Kaefferkopf Riesling comes from 60-year-old vines.

Domaine Pierre Adam

8 rue du Lieutenant Louis Mourier, 68770 Ammerschwihr

+33 3 89 78 23 07

Nathalie Adam

info@domaine-adam.com

www.domaine-adam.com

16 ha

[map p. 36]

Pierre and Simone Adam founded the domain in 1950 with just 1 ha of vines. Since then it has expanded considerably. The next generation, Rémy and Nathalie, took over in 1990. There's a new cellar an tasting room. The basic range, Vins de Tradition, comes from plots to the east of Ammerschwihr where the soils are sandy and pebbly. The Vins de Prestige come from three sites. Pinot Gris comes from lieu-dit Katzenstegel, a little higher on the slopes with granitic terroir; and there is also a second Pinot Gris aged in barriques. Kaefferkopf is the local grand cru at Ammerschwihr, and has Gewürztraminer and Riesling from terroir of calcareous clay. Grand cru Schlossberg, just to the north at Kaysersberg, also has Gewürztraminer and Riesling from granitic terroir. The Gewürztraminer is usually slightly sweet, with about 20 g/l residual sugar. There's also Pinot Noir aged in barriques.

Domaine Pierre Arnold

16 rue de la Paix, 67650 Dambach-la-Ville

+33 3 88 92 41 70

Pierre Arnold

alsace.pierre.arnold@orange.fr

www.vins-pierre-arnold.fr

8 ha; 45,000 bottles

[map p. 35]

The domain has been handed from father to son since 1711, and has been bottling its own wine since 1926. The present generation, Pierre and Suzanne Arnold, worked at Domaine Voarick in Burgundy for six years before taking over in 1986; their experience shows in the use of barriques for aging the Pinot Gris Cuvée du Tricentenaire. Otherwise the white wines are aged in stainless steel or foudres (Pinot Noir is aged in barriques). Vin Nature is a blend of 90% Riesling with 10% Auxerrois, aged for 9 months in stainless steel, and bottled unfined and unfiltered with minimal sulfur. The top holdings are in grand cru Frankstein, which produces Riesling, Pinot Gris, and Gewürztraminer from granitic terroir.

Domaine Laurent Bannwarth

9 Rue Principale, 68420 Obermorschwihr
+33 3 89 49 30 87
Régine Bannwarth
laurent@bannwarth.fr
www.bannwarth.fr

10 ha; 60,000 bottles
[map p. 37]

This is a very distinctive family domain. Created in the 1950s by Laurent Bannwarth, his son Stéphane now makes the wines, and the business side is run by Stéphane's wife Geneviève and sister Régine. Stéphane has moved the domain into the far reaches of natural winemaking with his range of Qvevri wines, made in thin-walled amphorae (less than 2 cm thick) from Georgia. The Qvevri project started in 2011. Winemaking in qvevri has some unusual features. Maceration is long, which means that most whites are effectively orange wines. Traditionally grapes are left in the amphorae for 6 months, but Stéphane has been experimenting with putting them in bags of fine mesh so they can be taken out sooner. The thin wall of the vessel combined with the porous character of the clay allows some exposure to oxygen. The qvevri are buried in the earth up to their necks. Winemaking is natural with no use of sulfites and no fining. The Qvevri wines are not bottled under cork, but under Vinolok, a reusable glass stopper. The Qvevri cuvées include Riesling, Gewürztraminer, Pinot Gris, and Auxerrois, as well as Synergie, a blend of the first three varieties. There are also other wines produced using Natural winemaking precepts, but fermented in normal containers, and some cuvées labeled Traditional that use more or less conventional winemaking.

Domaine Laurent Barth

3 rue du Maréchal de Lattre de Tassigny, 68630 Bennwihr
+33 3 89 47 96 06
Laurent Barth
laurent.barth@wanadoo.fr

4.5 ha; 25,000 bottles
[map p. 36]

After experience elsewhere, including the New World, Laurent Barth took over this small family domain in 1999, and started estate bottling in 2004. Most of the vineyards are around Bennwihr, with 28 parcels altogether. When Laurent replants plots, he uses very high vine density, up to 12,000 per hectare. Producing a variety of cuvées to represent different terroirs, he is known for a delicate style, and especially for Pinot Noir and for cuvées from grand cru Marckrain. The style tends to be dry: even the Pinot Gris from Marckrain is usually dry. Dry wines have minimal sulfur (just a little is added at bottling).

Domaine Baumann Zirgel

5 rue du Vignoble, 68630 Mittelwihr
+33 3 89 47 90 40
Benjamin Zirgel
baumann-zirgel@wanadoo.fr
www.baumann-zirgel.com

11 ha; 60,000 bottles
[map p. 36]

The domain was founded in 1953; Benjamin and Valérie Zirgel took over in 2008. Although this is a small domain, it has a large range, including wines from Riesling, Pinot Gris,. and Gewürztraminer from the lieu-dits Streng, Schwenkel, Stumpfgasse, and Bouxberg around Mittelwihr, and four grand crus, Mandelberg (Riesling and Gewürztraminer), Schlossberg and Schoenenbourg (Riesling), and Sporen (Gewürztraminer). There are also Crémant, Vendange Tardives, SGN, and Eaux-de-Vies. Wines to try are the Gewürztraminer from Sporen, the Riesling from Streng (not quite bone dry, with 5.8 g/l residual sugar), and the Pinot Noir Pièce de Chêne.

Domaine Charles Baur

29 Grand'rue, 68420 Eguisheim
+33 3 89 41 32 49
Armand Baur
cave@vinscharlesbaur.fr
www.vinscharlesbaur.fr

17 ha; 110,000 bottles [map p. 37]

The domain was founded in 1930. Since 2014 it has been managed by Armand Baur (grandson of the founder) and his son Arnaud. Most of the vineyards are around Eguisheim (including three grand crus), but there is also one plot farther south, and parcels to the north in grand cru Brand. Wine are aged in a mix of foudres and stainless steel. The house is known for its commitment to producing wines as dry as possible. The top wine is the Riesling from grand cru Eichberg. The cellars and tasting room are in the center of the village.

Cave de Beblenheim

1 route du Vin, 68980 Beblenheim
(shop); 14 rue de Hoen, 68980
Beblenheim (cellars)
+33 3 89 47 90 02
Patrick Aledo
info@cave-beblenheim.com
www.cave-beblenheim.com

520 ha; 5,000,000 bottles
[map p. 36]

The cooperative was founded in 1952, and is now the sixth largest producer in Alsace, with more than 180 members, many practicing viticulture by lutte raisonnée. The cellars are in the village (and can be visited by appointment), and there is a boutique on the route du Vin just outside (which is always open). There's a wide range of wines representing all varieties, mostly oriented towards entry level, as indicated by quite low prices, even for the grand crus. The style tends to be just off-dry for basic Riesling and distinctly sweet for grand crus; Pinot Gris and Gewürztraminer are usually sweet.

Domaine Pierre & Frédéric Becht

26, Faubourg-des-Vosges, 67120
Dorlisheim
+33 3 88 38 18 22
Pierre & Frédéric Becht
info@domaine-becht.com
www.domaine-becht.com

22 ha
[map p. 34]

Now under the fourth generation, this family domain is run by Pierre Becht and his son Frédéric. Located in the northern part of the appellation, vineyards are divided by Dorlisheim and the lieu-dit Stierkopf at Mutzig , five minutes to the northwest. Plantings include all the traditional varieties of Alsace, plus Chardonnay. Altogether there are 64 different wines. The basic range and the Stierkopf range both include all the varieties. Wines labeled Lieu-Dit Stierkopf are a notch up, and include a Pinot Auxerrois aged in barrique and Pinot Noir, aged in barriques for 10 months. There's a range of late-harvest wines, eaux de vie, and nine Crémants, ranging from Extra Brut to Demi-Sec. All wines are AOP Alsace: there are no grand crus.

Vins Jean Becker

4, Route d'Ostheim, 68340
Zellenberg
+33 3 89 47 90 16
Martine Becker
vinsbecker@orange.fr
www.vinsbecker.com

18 ha; 100,000 bottles
[map p. 36]

The estate has been passed from father to son since 1610. A negociant activity started in 1848. Between the first and second world wars, Becker supplied wine to Maison Nicolas. The production of wine under the domain name of Jean Becker started in 1968, and Jean-Philippe et Jean-François Becker is also used as a marque. Jean-Philippe is the winemaker, Jean-François looks after the vineyards, and Martin Becker runs the business. Two thirds of plantings are Riesling, Gewürztraminer, and Pinot Gris, and Pinot Noir is 15%. There are holdings in four grand crus: Froehn, Schoenenbourg, Schlossberg, and Sonnenglanz. The latest addition to the range is the Nature wines, which have no added sulfur. The wines have a very light style.

Domaine Jean Marc Bernhard

21 Grand Rue, 68230 Katzenthal
+33 3 89 27 05 34
Anne-Caroline et Frédéric Bernhard
vins@jeanmarcbernhard.fr
www.jeanmarcbernhard.fr

11.5 ha; 60,000 bottles [map p. 37]

The Bernhard family bought the property, which dates from the sixteenth century, in 1802, and is now in its ninth generation. Frédéric Bernhard succeeded his father at the start of the century. Unusually for a small family domain, holdings include a variety of grand crus, with a third of the vineyards in Schlossberg, Wineck Schlossberg, Furstentum, Kaefferkopf, Florimont, and Mambourg, giving the domain a preponderance of granitic terroirs. There is a complete range from Crémant and AOP Alsace varietals, to grand crus, to late harvest wines.

Domaine Émile Beyer

7 place du Château St Léon, 68420 Eguisheim
+33 3 89 41 40 45
Valérie & Christian Beyer
info@emile-beyer.fr
www.emile-beyer.fr

17 ha; 120,000 bottles [map p. 37]

Beyer split into two domains at the start of the nineteenth century, and Émile Beyer's tasting room is adjacent to Léon Beyer's in the center of Eguisheim, although the winery was moved in 2009 to a modern facility on the outskirts of the village. Christian Beyer is the fourteenth generation. Wines come from estate grapes, except for the Tradition range. Emile Beyer's vineyards are exclusively around Eguisheim, with a third in grand crus Eichberg or Pfersigberg. The pride of the domain is the 2.5 ha of Clos Lucas Beyer within Pfersigberg, originally purchased by Lucas Beyer in 1792, which Christian painstakingly reassembled in 2010; planted with Riesling lower down, and Pinot Noir at the top, its first vintage is 2020.

Domaine André Blanck et ses fils

Ancienne Cour-des-Chevaliers de Malte, 68240 Kientzheim
+33 3 89 78 24 72
Charles Blanck
charles.blanck@free.fr
www.andreblanck.com

15 ha; 90,000 bottles .map p. 36]

One of many Blanck families in Kientzheim, André Blanck can trace its involvement in wine back to 1675. Vineyards are around the village, with two thirds in grand crus Schlossberg and Furstentum or lieu-dits Altenbourg and Rosenbourg. Some of the vineyards were at one time the property of the Templiers de St-Jean de Jérusalem, which explains the name of the property in Kientzheim. The caves date from the sixteenth century. The Alsace Riesling is more or less dry, but most other cuvées are sweet, including the Alsace Pinot Gris and Gewürztraminer, and the Rieslings from Schlossberg.

Domaine Boeckel

2 rue de La Montagne, 67140 Mittelbergheim
+33 3 88 08 91 02
Thomas Boeckel
boeckel@boeckel-alsace.com
www.boeckel-alsace.com

24 ha; 300,000 bottles [map p. 34]

The family has been in Mittelbergheim since 1530, and Frédéric Boeckel started to sell the estate wines in 1853. Jean-Daniel and Thomas Boeckel are the fifth generation. Vineyards are around Mittelbergheim and the surrounding villages, including Zotzenberg (the local grand cru. Grapes are also purchased from another 15 ha from organic growers for the basic range. Wines age in very old 75 hl foudres. The range from the slopes around Mittelbergheim are called the Midelberg wines. The flagship wine is Sylvaner from grand cru Zotzenberg, which also produces cuvées in Riesling, Pinot Gris, and Gewurztraminer. A Pinot Noir, Les Terres Rouges, also comes from Zotzenberg.

Domaine Borès

15, lieu-dit Leh, 67140 Reichsfeld
+33 3 88 85 58 87
Marie-Claire & Pierre Borès
contact@domaine-bores.fr
domaine-bores.fr

10 ha
[map p. 35]

The domain is at the entrance to the tiny village of Reichsfeld, at the end of the road right in the Vosges, with some of the steepest slopes in the area. Marie-Claire and Pierre Borès established the domain in 1988 and are now helped by their daughter Marion. Most of the vineyards are on the schist of Schieferberg, with the rest on the sandstone of Sohlenberg. The entry-level range is called Les Intemporels, there are Sylvaner and Riesling from Sohlenberg, and Sylvaner, Muscat, Pinot Gris, and Riesling from Scheiferberg. The speciality is sweet wine, with Gewürztraminer Borès No. 12 as the top cuvée.

Maison Bott Frères

13, Avenue du Gal de Gaulle, 68150
Ribeauvillé
+33 3 89 73 22 50
Laurent Bott
info@bott-freres.fr
www.bott-freres.fr

20 ha; 150,000 bottles
[map p. 36]

The family started as a brewer before becoming a wine producer and negociant in 1835. The house is run today by Laurent and Nicole with their son Paul. The estate vineyards are mostly around Ribeauvillé. There's a complete range of wines, from Crémants, still wines from entry-level to grand crus, eaux-devies and liqueurs. Grand cru wines include Pinot Gris from Gloeckelberg, Gewürztraminer from Gloeckelberg, and Riesling from Osterberg, Geisberg, and Kirchberg de Ribeauvillé. Riesling Grand Trio was introduced in 2016 and is a blend from grand crus Osterberg, Geisberg, and Kirchberg de Ribeauvillé.

Domaine Brand et fils

13 rue de Wolxheim, 67120
Ergersheim
+33 3 88 38 17 71
Philippe Brand
domainebrand@gmail.com
www.domainebrand.fr

10 ha; 50,000 bottles
[map p. 34]

Located at the northern border of the wine region, about 15 miles to the west of Strasbourg, the domain was founded in 1956 by Lucien Brand, starting with polyculture and committing completely to viticulture only in the 1970s. Charles Brand took over and moved the domain into organic viticulture; then in 2006 his son Philippe joined, and in 2015 moved into biodynamics. The range of Vins Naturels includes 5 varietals and two blends (one is Pinot Blanc and Chardonnay; the other is an orange wine labeled Pinot Gris but including 20% Pinot Noir); these have no sulfites added, no fining, and no filtration. The Traditionnelle range of the major varieties from lieu-dit Kefferberg is produced to organic criteria, with a small amount of sulfur. There's also a small range of red wines from grapes purchased from growers in the south of France, but the wines are made in Alsace. The domain is into oenotourism, and Philippe organizes tastings and other events throughout the year.

Camille Braun & Fils

16, Grand'rue, 68500 Orschwihr
+33 3 89 76 95 20
Christophe Braun
cbraun@camille-braun.com
www.camille-braun.com

15 ha; 100,000 bottles [map p. 38]

The family has been in Alsace since 1583, making wine in Orschwihr since 1902, when Michel Braun bought a house in the center of the village. Camille Braun moved from polyculture to full time viticulture in 1960, then passing the domain on to her son, Christophe, in 1987. Vineyards are mostly around the village of Orschwihr, with the top wines coming from the grand cru of Pfingstberg and the lieu-dit Bollenberg, and also farther south in Uffholtz, from Christophe's wife Chantal. The style is conventional, which is to say that entry-level wines tend to be dry, except for Gewürztraminer, and wines from the grand crus often show some residual sugar, just detectable for Riesling, quite obvious for Pinot Gris and Gewürztraminer.

Paul Buecher et Fils

15 rue Sainte Gertrude, 68920 Wettolsheim
+33 3 89 80 64 73
Jérôme Buecher
vins@paul-buecher.com
www.paul-buecher.com

32 ha; 250,000 bottles [map p. 37]

The family has been in Wettolsheim since the seventeenth century. The estate took its present form as the result of a marriage uniting two domains in 1952; the estate had 5 ha at the time. The next generation moved into Crémant. Purchases of vineyards in grand crus Hengst, Sommerberg, and Brand were part of a move to quality in the 1990s. There are more than 50 parcels altogether. Jérôme Buecher took over as winemaker in 2002. The style tends to show a little residual sugar.

Domaine Ernest Burn

8, rue basse, 68420 Gueberschwihr
+33 3 89 49 20 68
Francis Burn
contact@domaine-burn.fr
www.domaine-burn.fr

10 ha; 40,000 bottles
[map p. 38]

This family domain has been in Gueberschwihr, at the southern end of the vineyards, for 350 years. The cellars date from 1623. Half of the holdings are in grand cru Goldert, including the monopole of Clos Saint Imer, which Ernest Burn reconstructed parcel by parcel in the 1940s. With a 60 degree slope in parts, it ripens a month later than other vineyards. The range from Clos St. Imer includes Riesling, Pinot Gris, and Gewürztraminer, but the domain is most famous for its Muscats in sweet styles from the grand cru.

Domaine Agathe Bursin

11 rue de Soultzmatt, 68250 Westhalten
+33 3 89 47 04 15
Agathe Bursin
agathe.bursin@wanadoo.fr

6 ha; 35,000 bottles [map p. 38]

Agathe Bursin started making wine in 2000 with 3 ha of vines inherited from her family. The domain may be small, but its vineyards are divided into 38 separate parcels, which encourages a focus on terroir-specific cuvées. A third of the holdings are in grand cru Zinnkoepflé. All wines are vinified exclusively in stainless steel. L'As de B is a cuvée from a 50-year-old plot in lieu-dit Bollenberg in which all the varieties are *complanté*. The other top wines are the Riesling and Pinot Gris from Zinnkoepflé, and the Pinot Noir from lieu-dit Strangenberg.

Joseph Cattin

35 rue Roger Frémeaux, 68420 Voegtlinshoffen
+33 3 89 49 30 21
Jacques Cattin
contact@cattin.fr
www.cattin.fr

70 ha; 2,500,000 bottles
[map p. 38]

This is one of the largest family-owned estates in Alsace. Vineyards extend from Colmar to the south, with the top holding in grand cru Hatschbourg. Jacques Cattin is especially proud to have resurrected Clos Madelon, at Steinbach in the south, by planting this abandoned *clos* of 8 ha with Pinot Gris in 2000. Not surprisingly for such a large estate, quality can be variable. Interest in the Rieslings starts with lieu-dit Eisbourg, only a touch below grand cru Hatschbourg, although the Cattins consider that their best terroir is a half hectare close to the winery that makes the Pur de Roche cuvée. The style is on the austere side.

Domaine Clé de Sol

6A rue du Cimetière, 68150
Ribeauvillé
+33 3 89 73 34 45
Simon Baltenweck
contact@domainecledesol.fr
www.domainecledesol.fr

3 ha; 10,000 bottles
[map p. 36]

This micro-domain originated in the division of a family estate in 1998. One half continues to send its grapes to the coop, but the Baltenwecks started to produce wine with a minimalist approach from their half. Even though the holding is small it is broken up, with each plot surrounded by fruit trees (including 120 varieties of old apple trees). Pressing is slow (using an old manual vertical press), and the juice is exposed to oxygen before fermentation, to ensure stability later. Winemaking is as natural as possible, with little or no use of sulfur, malolactic fermentation left to occur or not, and aging on the full lees in old barriques for Pinot Noir, Pinot Gris, Pinot Blanc, and Sylvaner, and stainless steel for Riesling and Gewürztraminer. The top wines are the Rieslings from grand crus Schlossberg and Rosacker.

Domaine Dock

20 Rue Principale, 67140
Heiligenstein
+33 3 88 08 02 69
Christian Dock
cdock@wanadoo.fr
www.domaine-dock-christian.fr

12 ha [map p. 35]

This family domain has been passed from father to son since 1879. Christian has been at the domain since 1980. Located at the village of Heiligenstein, on the slopes dominated by Mont Sainte-Odile, a speciality is the Klevener de Heiligenstein (coming from the rosé variety of Traminer). The cuvée here shows a golden color and is off-dry, with 18 g/l residual sugar. All the other varieties are produced, as well as eaux de vie.

Dopff Au Moulin

2 avenue Jacques Preiss, 68340
Riquewihr
+33 3 89 49 09 69
Étienne-Arnaud Dopff
domaines@dopff-au-moulin.fr
www.dopff-au-moulin.fr

70 ha; 1,600,000 bottles
[map p. 36]

Dopff is a very old name in Riquewihr, dating from 1574, and the family became wine merchants in the nineteenth century. Estate vineyards extend south from Riquewihr, but most production comes from purchased grapes: the house is one of the largest negociants in Alsace, purchasing grapes from more than 600 growers. The domain in its present form really dates from the early twentieth century, when Julien Dopff discovered Champagne, and then initiated the production of Crémant in Alsace, which remains a major focus of the house, representing half of production. There are more than ten different cuvées, including Blanc de Blancs, Blanc de Noirs, and several cuvées based on blends of Chardonnay, Pinot Noir, Pinot Blanc, and Auxerrois. Riesling and the other local varieties are confined to still wines, with a focus at the high end on the local grand cru, Schoenenbourg. Quality is typical for a large negociant.

Dopff & Irion

1, Cour du Château, BP 3, 68340
Riquewihr
+33 3 89 49 08 92
Laëtitia Rinaldo
contact@dopff-irion.com
www.dopff-irion.com

🚶 ⛏ 🍇 🛢 ⚲ ♺

32 ha; 200,000 bottles
[map p. 36]

You can hardly miss Dopff & Irion, in the Château de Riquewihr, right at the entrance to the village. The Dopff and Irion families go well back into Alsace history, and the estate was created in 1945 when René Dopff married the widowed Madame Irion. They took over the Château de Riquewihr and reconstructed the vineyards into four different estates, each focusing on a different variety. In addition to the vineyards at Riquewihr (from which the wines are labeled as Château de Riquewihr), subsequently they also purchased the Château d'Issenbourg and its 5 ha of vineyards farther south at Rouffach (wines are labeled as Clos Château d'Issenbourg). In addition the house is a negociant, labeling the wines simply as Dopff and Irion. In 1997, Dopff and Irion was sold to the cooperative at Pfaffenheim (whose wines are sold under the Pfaff label: see mini-profile), but continues to label wines under its own name. Quality is average.

Domaine Jean-Marc Dreyer

8 rue de la Marne, 67560 Rosheim
+33 3 88 48 06 93
Claudine Dreyer
jeanmarcdreyer@free.fr

🚶 ⛏ 🍇 ◗

6 ha; 20,000 bottles [map p. 34]

After Jean-Marc took over the family estate in 2003, he moved to an extreme form of biodynamic viticulture and natural winemaking. Jean-Marc learned natural winemaking with Patrick Meyer, one of the pioneers of natural wine in Alsace, and is committed to the point at which he says, "Natural winemaking is not at all the same thing as conventional viticulture, and the clients aren't the same either!" The winery is located in the northern part of the area, just by the walls of the fortified village of Rosheim, a little southwest of Strasbourg. Vineyards are broken up into 25 parcels around Rosheim. The white varietal wines in the ORIGIN series have 10-20 days skin contact, so they are well into the direction of orange wines. There are also some blends of varieties across vintages, with more conventional vinification after direct pressing. There are two Pinot Noirs, Elios, aged in foudres, and Anigma, aged in barriques. All wines are fermented as dry as possible, with fermentation often lasting right through the winter.

Domaine Fernand Engel

1 route du Vin, 68590 Rorschwihr
+33 3 89 73 77 27
Sandrine & Xavier Baril
info@fernand-engel.fr
www.fernand-engel.fr

🚶 ⛏ 🍇 🍇

60 ha; 400,000 bottles
[map p. 36]

Fernand Engel started making wine on a small scale at his parent-in-law's farm in 1949. He purchased his first vines in 1956, his son Bernard came into the domain in 1970, and in 1978 they built a winery at the entrance to the village. Bernard's daughter Sandrine and her husband Xavier Baril joined the domain in 1995 and have now taken over. The domain was extended in 2013 by purchasing the Domaine Freyburger at Bergheim. Vineyards extend altogether over more than 160 different parcels at Rorschwihr and Bergheim. The top holdings are in the grand crus Praelatenberg, Gloeckelberg, Mandelberg, and Altenberg de Bergheim. A large estate for Alsace, the domain produces an extensive range of all grape varieties from entry-level wines to sweet dessert wines. Visitors can taste the wines in a spacious tasting room with a panoramic view over the vineyards and the Plaine d'Alsace. The domain also uses the alternative label of Joseph Rudloff.

Domaine Vincent Fleith

8 lieu-dit Lange Matten, 68040
Ingersheim
+33 3 89 27 24 19
Vincent Fleith
contact@vincent-fleith.fr
www.vincent-fleith.fr

9 ha; 60,000 bottles
[map p. 37]

The family involvement in wine started in 1661. René Fleith established the estate with 4 ha in 1970 and started to sell his own wines in 1977. By 1996 when Vincent took over, after gaining experience in the New World, the domain had reached its present size. Most of the vineyards are around Ingersheim. Wines fall into several ranges: Tradition are varietal wines, mostly off-dry; Terroir are varietals from named lieu-dits and (except Gewürztraminer) are dry or close to dry; the Cuvées Speciales are selected lots of Riesling, Pinot Gris, Gewürztraminer, or Pinot Noir; and at the top comes Pinot Gris from grand cru Furstentum, and a range of vendange tardive and SGN.

Joseph Freudenreich & Fils

3 Cour Unterlinden, 68420
Eguisheim
+33 3 89 41 36 87
Marc Freudenrich
info@joseph-freudenreich.fr
www.joseph-freudenreich.fr

15 ha
[map p. 37]

The family has been in Eguisheim since the eighteenth century. Joseph Freudenreich created the domain in 1900. Marc Freudenreich started to make the wine in 1978, and took over the domain ten years later; his daughter Amélie joined him in 2015. Vineyards are mostly around Eguisheim, with smaller plots at Turckheim, Ammerschwihr, and Saint-Hippolyte. There is a full range of wines, with the top cuvées coming from grand crus Eichberg and Pfersigberg. The top Pinot Noir comes from the granitic terroir of Saint-Hippolyte. The style is not quite dry: the four Riesling cuvées, Alsace AOP, Vieilles Vignes, Eichberg, and Pfersigberg all have 7 g/l residual sugar. For Pinot Gris, sugar levels increase from Alsace AOP to grand cru; Gewürztraminer is perceptibly sweet.

Domaine Frey-Sohler

72 Rue de l'Ortenbourg, 67750
Scherwiller
+33 3 88 92 10 13
Damien Sohler
contact@frey-sohler.fr
www.frey-sohler.fr

29 ha; 160,000 bottles
[map p. 35]

A family affair, Frey-Sohler is run by brothers Damien (who looks after the business) and Nicolas (the winemaker). The estate goes back three hundred years in the village, and took its name in 1902 from Xavier Frey and his son-in-law Charles Sohler. Located just below the Château de l'Ortenbourg, vineyards are closely grouped but have several distinct terroirs: Rittersberg has very shallow soil on granite; l'Ortenbourg has deeper soils, also on granite; Scherwiller (one of the communal subappellations) has more alluvial soil; Kreffzen is very dry. The top holding is in grand cru Frankstein, on granite with mica, from which there is Gewürztraminer. There is the usual range of varietal wines, and in 2017 a blend was introduced to showcase the granitic terroir of Rittersberg, with 45% each of Riesling and Pinot Gris, and 10% of Gewürztraminer, in off-dry style.

Domaine Pierre Frick

5 Rue Baer, 68250 Pfaffenheim
+33 3 89 49 62 99
Chantal Frick
contact@pierrefrick.com
www.pierrefrick.com

12 ha; 70,000 bottles
[map p. 38]

The domain is considered to be one of the pioneers in biodynamic viticulture and natural winemaking in Alsace. The family has been making wine for twelve generations, and today Jean-Pierre Frick works with his son Thomas. The domain has been organic since 1970 and biodynamic since 1981. As they describe their approach, "we don't interfere in the cellar, we produce wines that are authentic, healthy, and living." Wines age in old oak foudres, and are bottled with minimal or no sulfur. In fact, today most of the cuvées are available as "zéro sulfite ajouté." But the approach is not hidebound: both corks and screwcaps have been rejected, and wines are bottled under a stainless steel cap, "to preserve purity." The top holdings are Riesling and Pinot Gris in grand cru Vorbourg, Riesling, Gewürztraminer, and Muscat in grand cru Steinert, and Gewürztraminer in grand cru Eichberg. An orange wine from Eichberg is called Pur Vin.

Domaine Henry Fuchs

8 rue du 3 Décembre, 68150
Ribeauvillé
+33 3 89 73 61 70
Paul Fuchs
contact@henryfuchs.fr
www.fuchs-henry-et-fils.fr

11 ha; 50,000 bottles
[map p. 36]

The estate was established in 1922 and has been bottling its own wines since 1945. The fourth generation, Paul Fuchs took over in 2005. Vineyards are fragmented, with many small plots. Vinification favors a dry style for Riesling, off-dry for Pinot Gris and Gewürztraminer. The top wines comes from a hectare in grand cru Kirchberg; another top Riesling comes from the 0.5 ha Hagel plot, high up above Kirchberg. There are also Pinot Gris, Gewürztraminer, and Pinot Noir from Kirchberg, and the domain is also known for its vieilles vignes Sylvaner from 65-year-old vines which ripen late in the Weinbaum lieu-dit.

Domaine Geschickt

1 Place de La Sinne, 68770
Ammerschwihr
+33 3 89 47 12 54
Frédéric & Christophe Geschickt
vignoble@geschickt.fr
www.geschickt.fr

12 ha
[map p. 36]

The estate was created by Bernadette Meyer and Jérôme Geschickt, who started bottling in 1955. Their son Frédéric took over in 1993, and his nephew Armand joined him in 2012. Unusually there are as many blended cuvées as varietals. Under Alsace AOP there are Riesling, Muscat, and Pinot Noir varietals, and PINO (a blend of Pinot Gris and Auxerrois), Le Schlouk (85% Gewürztraminer and 15% Sylvaner), Phenix (Pinot Gris and Gewürztraminer), and 6 Pieds sur Terre (both black and white varieties, with Pinot Noir, Pinot Gris, Auxerrois, Riesling, Muscat, and Gewürztraminer). All the wines are labeled Vin Nature. Aging is in very old foudres. From the grand crus, there is Kaefferkopf (a blend of 60% Gewürztraminer, 30% Riesling, and 10% Pinot Gris) and a pure Riesling; and there is a Riesling from Wineck-Schlossberg. There is also a range of Crémants and a Pet'Nat (sparkling wine made by the old method of one fermentation in bottle).

Domaine Pierre-Henri Ginglinger

33 Grand Rue, 68420 Eguisheim
+33 3 89 41 32 55
Mathieu Ginglinger
contact@vins-ginglinger.fr
www.vins-ginglinger.com

15 ha; 100,000 bottles
[map p. 37]

Located within the medieval village, this family domain dates from 1610. It had only just over a hectare when Henri Ginglinger took over in 1946, but has been steadily increased by each successive generation. Mathieu, who took over in 2001 is the twelfth generation. Vineyards extend over the villages of Eguisheim, Herrlisheim, and Wuenheim, with almost a third of the holdings in grand crus Eichberg (Riesling and Gewürztraminer), Pfersigberg (Pinot Gris and Gewürztraminer)), and (most recently) Ollwiller (Riesling and Pinot Gris). In addition to the regular range of varietals under AOP Alsace, Ambre is a blend of Auxerrois and Pinot Gris aged in demi-muid, St. Léon is a Gewürztraminer from 55-year-old vines, and there's an SGN ice wine from Gewürztraminer.

2 rue de l'École, 67140 Andlau
+33 3 88 08 95 88
Rémy Gresser
domaine@gresser.fr
www.gresser.fr

10.6 ha; 60,000 bottles
[map p. 35]

The Gressers have been making wine in Andlau since 1520. Having served as President of the CIVA, Rémy Gresser is a notable figure in the region. "I cultivate my vines in the same way as our ancestors," he says. All around Andlau, his holdings include grand crus with various terroirs, Kastelberg (the most mineral, from schist), Wiebelsberg (the most floral, from sandstone), and Moenchberg (the most opulent, from calcareous terroir). The style tends towards dry, although (for example) the Kritt Gewürztraminer (named for the gravel soils) is well into off-dry. The domain makes a point of keeping back wines so older vintages are available.

Domaine Gross

11, rue du Nord, 68420
Gueberschwihr
+33 3 89 49 24 49
Vincent Gross
contact@domainegross.fr
www.domainegross.fr

10 ha
[map p. 38]

Louis Gros founded the domain in 1956 with only 2.5 ha. His son Henri took over in due course, followed by his grandson Rémy in 1980; Rémy is now helped by his son, Vincent. Vineyards fall into six different terroirs, plus grand cru Goldert. In the entry-level range, Riesling is dry; other varieties may have a touch of residual sugar. In the Vins de Terroir range, from Rebgarten, Muscat, aged in stainless steel, is dry; Gewürztraminer and Pinot Gris, both aged in foudre, are sweet with 23 and 30 g/l residual sugar; and Gewürztraminer from Kastelweg is a little sweeter. Pinot Gris Christine is similar, but represents a selection from calcareous parcels. Pinot Gris Neueg also comes from calcareous terroir, but is dry. Riesling Steinberg, from calcareous terroir and sandstone, is dry. There is also a range called Macération, in which Muscat, Gewürztraminer, or Pinot Gris macerate with the skins for 25 days before pressing, followed by fermentation and aging in foudre: these are dry. From grand cu Goldert there are Riesling (dry), Gewürztraminer (sweet) and Muscat. There are several cuvées of Vendange Tardive and SGN, including Muscat and Gewürztraminer from Goldert.

Domaine Jean-Marie Haag

17 rue des Chèvres, 68570
Soultzmatt
+33 3 89 47 02 38
Jean-Marie Haag
info@domaine-haag.fr
www.domaine-haag.fr

7 ha; 50,000 bottles
[map p. 38]

The domain was founded in 1930, and has been in the hands of the third generation since 1982, remaining small enough that Myriam and Jean-Marie can undertake the viticulture themselves. Located in the warm area of the Vallée Noble, south of Colmar, its vineyards are in 36 separate plots in and around grand cru Zinnkoepflé. Gewürztraminer therefore ranks high, with Zinnkoepflé in the lead. Another notable site in the portfolio is lieu-dit Breitenberg, a south-facing hill planted with Pinot Gris.

Domaine Pierre Hering

6 rue du Docteur Sultzer, 67140
Barr
+33 3 88 08 90 07
Pierre & Jean-Daniel Hering
jdhering@wanadoo.fr
www.vins-hering.com

10 ha; 70,000 bottles
[map p. 35]

The Hering family has been making wine in Barr since 1858. Jean-Daniel has been in charge since 1971. Its most important vineyard is in grand cru Kirchberg, which represents half the domain and is planted with the top three varieties. There are also plots in two *clos* nearby, Clos de la Folie Marco planted with Riesling and Sylvaner, and the protected site of Clos Gaensbroennel known for late-harvest Gewürztraminer. Planted since 1998, lieu-dit Rosenegert, on the edge of Kirchberg, has five varieties intermingled (50% Riesling, smaller amounts of the others), with the intention of representing the place rather than any one variety.

Cave Vinicole De Hunawihr

48 Route de Ribeauvillé, 68150
Hunawihr
+33 3 89 73 61 67
François Bosch
boutique@cave-hunawihr.com
www.cave-hunawihr.com

200 ha; 2,000,000 bottles
[map p. 36]

The cooperative was founded in 1954 and now has 130 members. Vineyards are mostly on clay and Muschelkalk around Hunawihr, which has 80% of the plots, with others in Ribeauvillé, Riquewihr, and Zellenberg. One of the largest producers in the immediate area, the cooperative has 13 ha in grand crus, including Rosacker and Schoenenbourg. A quarter of production is exported. The range of wines is extensive, from Crémant, to generic AOP Alsace, to lieu-dits and grand crus, and vendange tardive. The coop is well into oenotourism and offers a guided walk around Rosacker once a week in the summer.

Domaine Armand Hurst

8 rue de La Chapelle, 68230
Turckheim
+33 3 89 27 40 22
Samuel Tottoli
domaine@armand-hurst.fr
www.hurst-shop.fr

12.5 ha; 80,000 bottles
[map p. 37]

The domain was founded in 1928. Armand took over in 1989 and moved the domain in 1991 to modern premises just outside the village, but the old foudres came with to the new winery. A major change occurred in 2016 when Marc Rinaldi invested in the domain and became a part owner. The domain has very impressive holdings, with more than half (7 ha) in grand cru Brand. There are cuvées of Riesling, Gewürztraminer, Pinot Gris, and Muscat from Brand in both regular and vendange tardive styles. The other cuvées of note are the Turckheim Riesling and Gewürztraminer.

Domaine André Kientzler

50 Route de Bergheim, 68150
Ribeauvillé
+33 3 89 73 67 10
Éric Kientzler
domaine@vinskientzler.com
www.vinskientzler.com

14 ha; 80,000 bottles
[map p. 36]

Now in its fifth generation, Kientzler is a highly praised winery, housed in a modern building with a tasting room just off main road outside Ribeauvillé. The coteaux of vineyards rises up opposite. "We look for berries at maturity not sur-maturity. We try to make wines that have a dry balance," says Eric Kientzler. Do they always have the same character? "No it is a matter of balance." Fermentation and élevage are in stainless steel, and last up to five months. All of the white varieties are produced, with about 20 cuvées in all. The varietal wines are workmanlike, but where the excitement comes is with the grand crus, about a third of the vineyards. The Geisberg Riesling seems to me to be far and away the best of Kientzler's wines.

Baron Kirmann

2 rue du Général de Gaulle, 67560
Rosheim
+33 3 88 50 43 01
Philippe & Corinne Kirmann
info@baronkirmann.com
www.baronkirmann.com

11 ha [map p. 34]

Kirmann's have been growing vines since 1768, and the domain itself dates from 1860, named for an ancestor who was made a Baron by Napoleon. Philippe Kirmann took over in 1993. Vineyards are on the calcareous-clay slopes around Rosheim, in the northern part of the appellation. There is a focus on Pinot Noir, with a basic wine, the Oberer Altenberg cuvée, and the Fût de Chêne, which ages in new barriques for 14 months. There is also a Crémant Blanc de Noirs. All wines are AOP Alsace: there are no grand crus.

Domaine Kirmann

6 rue-des-Alliés, 67680 Epfig
+33 3 88 85 59 07
Olivier Kirmann
domaine@kirmann.com
www.kirmann.com

7.5 ha; 35,000 bottles
[map p. 35]

Olivier Kirmann is the third generation at this family estate, and has expanded to open a restaurant at the domain serving traditional Alsatian cuisine. In addition to the range of varietal wines under AOP Alsace, there's a line of Vieilles Vignes, all from vines over 35-years-old, in selected plots; usually dry, these give the best impression of the domain. There is only one grand cru cuvée, Riesling from Frankstein, where the style can vary considerably with vintage: 2014 is dry, but 2011 is sweet.

Klée Frères

18 Grand'rue, 68230 Katzenthal
+33 3 89 27 39 34
Francis Klee
info@klee-freres.com
www.klee-freres.com

2 ha; 10,000 bottles
[map p. 37]

Victor Klee was the village baker and also looked after the family vineyards after the second world war. His three sons, Francis, Gérard, and Laurent are in charge today at this small family domain, with Francis making the wine. Vineyards are south of the village, with the top holding in the grand cru Kaefferkopf. The small range includes Edelzwicker and another blended wine, Riesling, Pinot Gris, Gewürztraminer, and Pinot Noir under Alsace AOP, and Riesling from Kaefferkopf. The style usually shows some sweetness.

André Kleinknecht

45 rue Principale, 67140
Mittelbergheim
+33 3 88 08 49 46
André Kleinknecht
andre.kleinknecht@wanadoo.fr

9 ha; 30,000 bottles
[map p. 34]

The domain is centered on Mittelbergheim, with vineyards running along the west side of the village. André's objective is to make wines as naturally as possible (which means minimal or zero sulfur) and as dry as possible. The top vineyards are the Kirchberg de Barr grand cru north of the village, where Riesling and Gewürztraminer are planted, and also a plot of Pinot Noir (for the "K" cuvée). Zotzenberg grand cru is west of the village, and has Sylvaner and Pinot Gris. The Rebbuhl lieu-dit is in Andlau and is planted with Pinot Blanc and Auxerrois which go into Crémant. White wines are aged for two years in old foudres.

Maison Klipfel

10 Rue des Jardins, 67140 Barr
+33 3 88 58 59 00
alsacewine@klipfel.com
www.klipfel.com

40 ha; 1,500,000 bottles
[map p. 35]

Maison Klipfel is nominally a medium-sized family estate, created in 1824 by Martin Klipfel. After André Lorentz, son of negociant Gustav Lorentz in Bergheim, married into the family in the 1950s, he ran the Maison in conjunction with a negociant activity. His son Jean-Louis Lorentz-Klipfel ran Maison Klipfel and the André Lorentz negociant until they were sold in 2016 after André's death at age 83 to the Helfrich family, who started in 1979 by producing Crémant in Alsace, and now own two other domains in Alsace, Domaine Moillard in Burgundy, and a range of properties elsewhere in France. Maison Klipfel's top holdings are 14 ha in grand crus Kirchberg, Wiebelsberg, and Kastelberg, including the 3.5 ha plot of Clos Zisser in Kirchberg, which Martin Klipfel purchased in 1830. Klipfel is known for aging its wines in very old foudres.

Vignoble Klur

105, rue des Trois-Épis, 68230
Katzenthal
+33 3 89 80 94 29
Clément Klur
info@klur.net
www.klur.net

1.6 ha; 5,000 bottles [map p. 37]

The Klur family has been in Katzenthal since the seventeenth century, but Clément created his own domain in 1999. "It's the smallest biodynamic domain in Alsace," he says. Vineyards are mostly on granite-based steep slopes. There's an air of enterprise here, with a bistro and accommodation. The Katz range is entry-level for several varieties, while wines marked Klur indicate origins in specific terroirs, including grand cru Winneck-Schlossberg. The domain has old vintages available.

Domaine René & Michel Koch

5 rue de La Fontaine, 67680
Nothalten
+33 3 88 92 41 03
René & Michel Koch
contact@vin-koch.fr
www.vin-koch.fr

12 ha [map p. 35]

This family domain goes back several generations. Georges Koch started bottling wine in 1958. His son René took over in 1970, and his son Michel joined him in 1996 and took over in 2006. Vineyards are around the village of Nothalten (south of Barr), all within a couple of miles of the winery. The entry-level range has all seven varieties. From specific terroirs, there are Sylvaner from lieu-dit Zellberg, Riesling from Heissenberg, and Pinot Noir from the granitic soils of Winzenberg and Heissenberg. The top wines are the Riesling and Pinot Gris from grand cru Muenchberg. There are also Vendange Tardive from Gewürztraminer, Pinot Gris, Riesling, and Muscat, and SGN, and Crémant.

Maison Kuentz-Bas

14 route-des-Vins, 68420 Husseren
les Châteaux
+33 3 89 49 30 24
Olivier Raffin
info@kuentz-bas.fr
www.kuentz-bas.fr

9 ha; 60,000 bottles
[map p. 37]

Founded in 1795 by the Kuentz family, and taking its present name after a marriage between the Kuentz and Bas families in 1895, this old house stayed in the Bas family until it was taken over by Jean-Baptiste Adam (see mini-profile) in 2004. Jean-Baptiste reduced yields and turned to organic viticulture to improve quality. The Trois Châteaux range identifies wines from estate vineyards, which are biodynamic. The top wines come from Eichberg and Pfersigberg grand crus.

Jacques & Christophe Lindenlaub

6 Faubourg-des-Vosges, 67120
Dorlisheim
+33 3 88 38 21 78
Christophe Lindenlaub
contact@vins-lindenlaub.com
www.vins-lindenlaub.com

12 ha; 70,000 bottles
[map p. 34]

At the northern border of the region, just west of Strasbourg, the Lindenlaub family has been making wines since 1759. The Zen ENSO circle is the motif on the label, intended to indicate the energy of the domain since Christophe joined his father, and many of the cuvées have names suggesting the approach of the domain, such as À griffes acérées (sharp claws) for the Riesling). Vineyards are dispersed around the local hills, mostly on clay-limestone terroir. Vinification is mostly in stainless steel. There are orange wines, which have 2-3 weeks maceration, from Gewürztraminer, Riesling, and Auxerrois. The top Riesling, and the Pinot Noir, come from lieu-dit Stierkopf.

Clément Lissner

16 rue de Strasbourg, 67120
Wolxheim
+33 3 88 38 10 31
Théo Schloegel
clement.lissner@wanadoo.fr
lissner.fr

10 ha; 35,000 bottles
[map p. 34]

Bruno Schloegel took over the domain in 2002 after the death of his uncle, Clément. He had previously been working as a wine consultant, and expanded the domain from its initial 2 ha. The viticultural approach is summarized by Bruno saying that, "the vines know better than us how to make ripe fruit." The top vineyard is a hectare on the grand cru Altenberg de Wolxheim, planted with Riesling, Gewürztraminer, and Muscat. Most of the wines are dry (although not necessarily bone dry). Aging is in either foudres or stainless steel, except for cuvées of Sylvaner and Pinot Gris that ferment and age in demi-muids, or barriques for Pinot Noir.

Domaine Loew

28 rue Birris, 67310 Westhoffen
+33 3 88 50 59 19
Étienne Loew
domaine.loew@orange.fr
domaineloew.fr

12 ha; 50,000 bottles
[map p. 34]

One of the few vignerons of the far northern part of the region, not far from Strasbourg, the domain is located around a courtyard behind an unassuming entrance in the road through Westhoffen. The estate dates from the eighteenth century, and Étienne Loew took over in 1996. At the time, most of the grapes were sold to the cooperative. The style is relatively light, from spicy Sylvaner, racy Riesling, to slightly phenolic Gewürztraminer: there's a distinct step up from the regular cuvées to the single vineyard cuvées. The style tends to be off-dry.

Maison Gustave Lorentz
91 rue des Vignerons, 68750
Bergheim
+33 3 89 73 22 22
Georges Lorentz
info@gustavelorentz.com
www.gustavelorentz.com

33 ha; 1,500,000 bottles
[map p. 36]

The family has been making wine here since 1836 — Georges is the fifth generation — but the negociant activity is far more important than the domain. In addition to the estate vineyards, the domain controls another 120 ha. Grapes tend to be purchased from the local region around Bergheim. The best wines come from the estate production, especially the plots in grand crus Kanzlerberg and Altenberg de Bergheim (the largest holding at 12 ha). Vinification takes a modern approach, indicated by the use of screwcaps.

Vignoble des 2 Lunes
21 rue Sainte-Gertrude, 68920
Wettolsheim
+33 3 89 30 12 80
Amélie & Cécile Buecher
contact@2lunes.fr
www.vignobledes2lunes.fr

14 ha
[map p. 37]

This family domain goes back seven generations and has been run since 2009 by Amélie and Cécile Buecher, both with degrees in oenology, Amélie making the wine and Cécile managing the domain. Vineyards are spread over six villages. The sisters are known for the lightness of their Crémants, which are zero dosage, including the Clair de Lune Blanc de Noirs. Most wines are aged in stainless steel or concrete, but Pinot Blanc and Riesling are aged in large foudres, as is the Pinot Noir. The range includes 25 wines altogether. The top holdings are in grand crus Hengst and Hatschbourg, planted with Pinot Gris. The style tends to off-dry.

Domaine Mader
68150 13 Grand-Rue, Hunawihr
+33 3 89 73 80 32
Jérôme Mader
vins.mader@laposte.net
www.vins-mader.com

11 ha; 55,000 bottles
[map p. 36]

The domain as such started when Jean-Luc left the cooperative in 1981 and started to bottle his own wine. His son Jérôme has been in charge since 2005. A good guide to the style is the sign in the cellar window: 'nos vins sont sec' (our wines are dry). The top holdings are just under a hectare in grand cru Rosacker (Riesling and Gewürztraminer) and a half hectare on grand cru Schlossberg (Pinot Gris). Riesling cuvees also come from lieu-dits Haguenau and Muhlforst (in Ribeauvillé), and the Alsace Riesling cuvée contains about 15% declassified fruit from Rosacker. Wines age in stainless steel.

Domaine du Manoir
56 rue de La Promenade, 68040
Ingersheim
+33 3 89 27 23 69
Marina Thomann
domainedumanoir@gmail.com
domainedumanoir.fr
9 ha; 20,000 bottles
[map p. 37]

Labels carry both the name of the domain and its location, Clos du Letzenberg, reflecting its origins when Marina and Jean-Francis Thomann replanted the slopes at Letzenberg in 1979 that had been abandoned since 1914. Surrounded by stone walls, the property is a monopole, and a genuine *clos*. It's very much a family affair, with everyone involved down to third generation winemaker Jean-Victor Thomann. The range of wines is not quite typical for the area. There's a single Riesling, Gewürztraminer comes in regular and late harvest styles, and there are 4 cuvées of Pinot Gris (Letzenberg is the regular cuvée, Cuvée Victoria is intended to be more Burgundian, and there are vendange tardive and SGN), and two Pinot Noirs.

Domaine Frédéric Mochel

56 Rue Principale, 67310
Traenheim
+33 3 88 50 38 67
Guillaume Mochel
contact@mochel.alsace
www.mochel.alsace

10 ha; 70,000 bottles
[map p. 34]

This is one of the relatively few domains in the far north of the appellation (just west of Strasbourg) to produce its own wines rather than send grapes to the cooperative. The family has been in Traenheim since 1669, the domaine converted from polyculture to excusive viticulture in 1967, and Guillaume Mochel has been in charge since 2001. Half of the vineyards are in grand cru Altenberg de Bergbieten, producing Riesling and Gewürztraminer. Trovium is a unusual blend of 70% Pinot Gris and 30% Pinot Blanc, aged in barriques after going through malolactic fermentation. Otherwise the wines age in large foudres.

Domaine Moltès

8-10 Rue du Fossé, 68250
Pfaffenheim
+33 3 89 49 60 85
Mickaël & Stéphane Moltès
domaine@vin-moltes.com
www.vin-moltes.com

25 ha
[map p. 38]

The domain was founded in 1930 by Antoine Moltès. Since his grandchildren, Mickaël and Stéphane took over in 1995, they have expanded the estate from 17 ha, built a new winery, and added a negociant activity to expand the range. The entry-level range, Tradition, comes from, vineyards at the base of the slopes around Pfaffenheim. The Terroir range comes from clay-limestone soils higher up the slopes, and including Riesling, Pinot Gris and Gewürztraminer (both perceptibly sweet), and Pinot Noir. Grand cru wines include Pinot Gris and Gewürztraminer from Steinert, and Gewürztraminer from Zinnkoepflé.

Domaine Neumeyer

29 rue Ettore Bugatti, 67120
Molsheim
+33 3 88 38 12 45
Jérôme Neumeyer
domaine.neumeyer@wanadoo.fr
www.vinsalsace.com/domaine-
neumeyer

16.5 ha; 70,000 bottles
[map p. 34]

Located by the fortified village of Molsheim (known for the Ettore Bugatti car museum), Xavier Neumeyer grew vines on a couple of hectares in the first part of the twentieth century. After the second world war, his son, Lucien, moved into viticulture and sent his grapes to the coop. The third generation, Gérard, studied in Beaune and joined the domain in 1976, building a winery to the west of the village, and slowly expanding the domain. Gérard ran the domain until handing over recently to his children Marie and Jérôme. The top wines comes from grand cru Bruderthal, close to the domain, where a holding of 3.5 ha is the domain's flagship and is planted with Riesling, Pinot Gris, and Gewürztraminer. Another top Riesling comes from lieu-dit Finkenberg of Avolsheim, where the soil is marl-limestone like Bruderthal. Wines are aged in old foudres.

Vins Gérard Nicollet

33 rue de la Vallée, 68570
Soultzmatt
+33 3 89 47 03 90
Marc Nicollet
vinsnicollet@wanadoo.fr
www.vins-nicollet.fr

14 ha [map p. 38]

This old domain took its modern form when it was reconstituted after phylloxera in the 1920s. Gérard started estate-bottling in 1965. Marc took over in 2004. Vines are spread out over around fifty different plots around Soulzmatt in the Vallée Noble, a few miles south of Colmar, including 2 ha in grand cru Zinnkoepflé. The entry-level range, Selection, tends to be relatively sweet. There are Pinot Gris, Gewürztraminer, and Riesling from Zinnkoepflé, again following the trend to significant residual sugar, leading into a range of Vendange Tardives and SGN.

Domaine de l'Oriel

133 rue des Trois-Épis, 68230
Niedermorschwihr
+33 3 89 27 40 55
Claude Weinzorn
oriel.weinzorn@sfr.fr
www.domaine-oriel.fr

9 ha; 40,000 bottles [map p. 37]

Claude is the thirteenth generation in the Weinzorn family to make wine in the tiny village of Niedermorschwihr. Claude took over in 1995 after his father's death in an accident in the vineyard—the steep vineyards are very difficult to work. Although small, the domain has plots in three grand crus, Sommerberg (the major grand cru holding of 3 ha), Brand, and a tiny holding in Florimont, on which the domain's reputation rests, especially Sommerberg (where Riesling is king).

Cave des Vignerons de Pfaffenheim

5 Rue Chai, 68250 Pfaffenheim
+33 3 89 78 08 08
Jean-Luc Hanauer
cave@pfaffenheim.com
www.pfaffenheim.com

320 ha; 2,500,000 bottles
[map p. 38]

Modernizing its image, this old cooperative, founded in 1957, and enlarged by merging in the late sixties with the coop at Gueberschwihr, now bottles its wines under the label Pfaff. Its 180 members have to agree to manual harvest to ensure quality (mechanical harvesting is common in Alsace). Vineyards are mostly on calcareous terroir. White wines are made exclusively in stainless steel. In addition to the wide range of wines, there is a range of Eau-de-Vies. In 1997 the coop took over Dopff and Irion (see mini-profile), which continues to function as an independent label. It size makes it one of the most important producers in Alsace.

Domaine Pfister

53 rue Principale, 67310
Dahlenheim
+33 3 88 50 66 32
Mélanie Pfister
vins@domaine-pfister.com
www.domaine-pfister.com

10 ha; 60,000 bottles [map p. 34]

Located at the northern boundary of the AOP, near Strasbourg, the domain dates from 1780. André Pfister took over in 1972, and his daughter Mélanie has been taking over since 2008. A new winery was built in 2011. Vineyards are fragmented into 40 parcels, but all within a couple of miles of the domain. Riesling represents a quarter of plantings. The style is committed to bone dry, with the best wines coming from grand cru Engelberg, notably Riesling and Gewürztraminer.

Domaine Edmond Rentz

7 Route du Vin, 68340 Zellenberg
+33 3 89 47 90 17
Patrick Rentz
info@edmondrentz.com
www.edmondrentz.com

27 ha
[map p. 36]

The estate dates from 1785 and has been bottling its wine since 1936. Patrick Rentz and his sister Catherine took over in 1995. Vineyards are in five communes in the center of the area: Bergheim, Ribeauvillé, Hunawihr, Zellenberg, and Riquewihr. The entry-level range includes all seven varieties. There are wines from four lieu-dits and three grand crus. Pinot Gris comes from calcareous-clay of Les Murets, at 270-350m altitude; Gewürztraminer comes from the steep limestone slopes of Rotenburg; Riesling comes from the clay-limestone slopes of Les Comtes; Pinot Noir comes from Zellenberg (near grand cru Froehn). The grand crus are Froehn (Gewürztraminer), Sonnenglanz (Pinot Gris, usually sweet with 32 g/l residual sugar), and Schoenenbourg (Riesling).

Vignoble du Rêveur

2 rue de la Cave, 68630 Bennwihr
+33 6 63 18 54 58
Mathieu Deiss & Emmanuelle
Milan
contact@vignoble-reveur.fr
www.vignoble-reveur.fr

7 ha; 40,000 bottles
[map p. 36]

Mathieu Deiss has been making the wine with his father at Domaine Marcel Deiss (see profile) since 2008, but in 2013 also started to make wine at his own domain with vineyards he inherited from his grandfather and uncle. The vineyards are mostly around Bennwihr; the wines are made at Marcel Deiss as, "I simply cannot be in two places at once during harvest. " The cuvées all somewhat follow the precepts of natural winemaking. Singulier comes from carbonic maceration of Riesling and Pinot, Vibrations is Riesling vinified in foudre with minimal intervention, Pierres Sauvages is Pinot Blanc made the same way, La Vie en Rose is Gewürztraminer vinified in stainless steel, Un Instant sur Terre is a blend of Gewürztraminer and Pinot Gris vinified in amphora, Artisan is an orange wine from the same blend vinified in stainless steel. All are dry.

Cave de Ribeauvillé

2 Route de Colmar, 68150
Ribeauvillé
+33 3 89 73 61 80
Yves Baltenweck
cave@cave-ribeauville.com
www.vins-ribeauville.com

265 ha; 2,000,000 bottles
[map p. 36]

One of the oldest cooperatives in France, founded in 1895, this is the best cooperative in Alsace, drawing on a great variety of terroirs, with ten grand crus and many notable lieu-dits. A sign of its serious approach is that it only accepts grapes harvested manually, and members must commit to providing it with their entire crop. Some of the cuvées are organic. It's a measure of success that the parking lot is always busy with people visiting the tasting room or taking out purchases from the shop.

Domaine Rieflé-Landmann

7 rue du Drotfeld, 68250
Pfaffenheim Fleurie
+33 3 89 78 52 21
Jean-Claude Rieflé
rieflé@riefle.com
www.riefle.com

23 ha; 160,000 bottles
[map p. 38]

Dating back to 1830, Domaine Rieflé expanded significantly when it purchased the vineyards of the well-regarded Domaine Seppi Landmann in 2011, extending their holdings farther along the Vallée Noble. (Seppi Landmann wines are still available in the market.) Under the combined name, Jean-Claude Rieflé is the winemaker, and his sons Thomas and Paul manage the vineyards and the business, respectively. The domain is located in an old house in the village of Pfaffenheim. Vineyards are fragmented into 79 parcels north of Rouffach. There are cuvées from several lieu-dits and from grand crus Steinert and Zinnkoepflé (part of the old Seppi Landmann holdings). The Rieslings are usually dry, or very close to it, with a tendency towards salinity. There is also Sylvaner. "It was almost eliminated in the 1970s," says Paul, "but now these are our oldest vines in Zinnkoepflé. It's magnificent, but we can't sell it as grand cru."

Domaine Rietsch

32 rue Principale, 67140
Mittelbergheim
+33 3 88 08 00 64
Jean-Pierre Rietsch
contact@alsace-rietsch.eu
alsace-rietsch.eu

12 ha; 50,000 bottles
[map p. 34]

The family has been in Mittelbergheim since the seventeenth century, involved with ancillary activities linked to wine, and the domain was created by Pierre and Doris Rietsch at the end of the 1970s. Their son Jean-Pierre has been involved since 1987 and now makes the wine. Winemaking is "natural:" very slow pressing and fermentation (which can last several months), aging in foudres, and bottling with minimal sulfur. In addition to the conventional cuvées there are "vins d'experimentation:" orange wines resulting from skin maceration for the more aromatic varieties, and a "cuvée perpétuelle" from Klevner (Savagnin rosé) based on a solera system. The top Rieslings come from grand crus Wiebelsberg and Zotzenberg, which also produces a Sylvaner. The entire range is usually dry (aided by the production of orange wines for Muscat, Gewürztraminer, and Pinot Gris.) The funky labels give a good idea of the idiosyncratic approach.

Domaine Catherine Riss

43 rue de la Montagne, 67140
Mittelbergheim
+33 3 90 57 48 99
Catherine Riss
catherine.riss@wanadoo.fr

4 ha; 12,000 bottles
[map p. 34]

The domain is unusual: a new venture rather than the continuation of an old estate. Catherine Riss's family has a restaurant to the east of the appellation: she qualified in winemaking in Burgundy and then worked at various wineries until winding up at Chapoutier in Alsace. She started her own domain with just over a hectare in 2012, making the wine at Lucas Reiffel's domain until she got her own facility in Bernardvillé. She expanded the domain to its present size in 2018, with 10 parcels dispersed around the village of Reichsfeld, just south of Andlau. Cuvées haven't really settled down yet, but have included conventional Rieslings, an Auxerrois-Sylvaner blend, a Pinot Noir-Gewürztraminer blend (labeled as Vin de France), and a Pinot Noir. The whimsical labels (drawn by a local artist) and names for the wines typify the originality of the approach.

Domaine Éric Rominger

16 rue Saint Blaise, 68250
Westhalten
+33 3 89 47 68 60
Claudine Rominger
vins-rominger.eric@orange.fr
domainerominger.fr

12 ha; 70,000 bottles
[map p. 38]

The estate was established relatively recently in 1970 in Bergholz by Armand Rominger. His son Éric took over in 1986 and moved the domain up the valley to Westhalten. Since Éric's death in 2014, his widow Claudine has managed the estate. The pride of the domain is its 5 ha holding in grand cru Zinnkoepflé, from which come Riesling, Pinot Gris, several cuvées of Gewürztraminer, and Sylvaner cuvée "Z." Les Sinneles is a Gewürztraminer from a single plot on Zinnkoepflé. The style tends to show a little residual sugar.

Vins Robert Roth

38A route Jungholtz, 68360 Soultz
Haut Rhin
+33 3 89 76 80 45
Christophe & Patrick Roth
domaine-robertroth@orange.fr
www.vinsroth.fr

14 ha [map p. 38]

Brothers Christophe and Patrick Roth have been in charge at this family domain since they took over from their father Robert in 1986. Located at the southern end of the appellation, the estate dates from the nineteenth century, and has been housed in its present cellars, on the outskirts of the town, since 1972; a new tasting room was added in 2015. The entry-level range is called Les Terres de Grès, reflecting the local terroir of grès (sandstone), and there are wines from two lieu-dits, Orschwillerbourg (clay and sandstone) and Mittelbourg (calcareous).

Domaine Daniel Ruff

64 rue Principale, 67140
Heiligenstein
+33 3 88 08 10 81
Daniel Ruff
ruffvigneron@wanadoo.fr
www.ruffvigneron.fr

15 ha [map p. 35]

Focused on vineyards around Heiligenstein, the family estate has been growing grapes since 1886, and has passed the domain from father to son for four generations. The range includes the usual varieties, but is unusual in presenting several cuvées of Klevener (a rosé variant related to Gewürztraminer), which is a local specialty in Heiligenstein. There's a village wine, a Vieilles Vignes from lieu-dit Schwendehiesel, and the cuvée l'Authentique, with sweetness increasing along the series from off-dry to semi-sweet.

Domaine Saint-Rémy Ehrhart

34 route d'Eguisheim, 68920
Wettolsheim
+33 3 89 80 60 57
Philippe & Corinne Ehrhart
vins@domainesaintremy.com
www.domaine-saint-remy.com

24 ha; 150,000 bottles
[map p. 37]

The domain has been handed from father to son since 1725, and since 1988 has been run by Philippe and Corinne Ehrhart. The next generation, Florian and Margot, are now involved. The domain moved into a new winery and tasting room on the edge of the village in 2014. Vineyards are dispersed over eleven villages around and south of Colmar, and include holdings in lieu-dits Rosenberg and Herrenweg, and four grand crus, Hengst (Riesling and Gewürztraminer), Brand (pinot Gris), Goldert (Gewürztraminer), and Schlossberg.

Julien Schaal

35 route du Vin, 68590 Saint
Hippolyte
+33 6 10 89 72 14
Julien Schaal
julien@vins-schaal.com
www.julienschaal.com

12 ha; 60,000 bottles
[map p. 36]

This unusual venture is essentially a micro-negociant started by Julien Schaal, who comes from Alsace, but now splits his time between making Riesling there in the summer, and making Chardonnay in South Africa in the winter. Alsace cuvées come from six grand crus, labeled according to the type of terroir: Schist for Kastelberg, Granite for Sommerberg, Calcaire for Rosacker, Gypsum for Schoenenbourg, Volcanique for Rangen, Contemplation for the red clay of Altenberg de Bergheim. The range offers an unusual opportunity to compare wines from north to south made by the same winemaker.

Schaeffer-Woerly

3 Place du Marché, 67650
Dambach-La-Ville
+33 3 88 92 40 81
Maxime Woerly
info@schaeffer-woerly.fr
www.schaeffer-woerly.com

8 ha; 50,000 bottles
[map p. 35]

Lucie and Vincent Woerly took over her family domain (previously called Schaeffer Robert) in 1987. Now their son Maxime is making the wine. Located in the center of the village, the cellars under the family house date from the seventeenth century. (An old press from the seventeenth century is in the tasting room.) Most of the vineyards are around the village of Dambach—the domain has doubled in size in the last thirty years—with the top holding of just under a hectare in grand cru Frankstein (producing dry Riesling, off-dry Pinot Gris, and sweet Gewürztraminer). Wines are aged in a mix of stainless steel and foudres.

Domaine Joseph Scharsch

12 Rue de l'Église, 67120 Wolxheim
+33 3 88 38 30 61
Nicolas Scharsch
cave@domaine-scharsch.com
www.domaine-scharsch.com

12 ha
[map p. 34]

The origins of the Scharsch family go back to 1755. In the first half of the twentieth century, the domain grew grapes as part of polyculture. After Joseph took over in 1972, he moved the domain into viticulture and begin estate-bottling. Nicolas, who joined his father in 1997 and took over in 2011, is the eighth generation. The domain is located in the north of the appellation, with its 35 parcels in the area known as the Couronne d'Or (Crown of Gold). Riesling is confined to the top parcels, and occupies 3.5 ha of plantings. The top wine is the Riesling Grand Cru Altenberg de Wolxheim. Other cuvées of note include the single-vineyard wines, Pinot Gris Noé and Clos St Materne, and Gewürztraminer Manon from limestone terroir. The Pinot Noir Les Petits Grains comes from two plots and ages in barriques with 20% new oak for 10 months. L'Ephémère is an unusual blend of Pinot Gris and Riesling which has no added sulfur.

Domaine Jean-Paul Schmitt

Hühnelmühle, 67750 Scherwiller
+33 3 88 82 34 74
Jean-Paul Schmitt
vins-schmitt@orange.fr
www.vins-schmitt.com

8 ha; 40,000 bottles [map p. 35]

Jean-Paul took over this family estate in 1983, and was joined by his son Bernd in 2003. Vineyards are unusually in a single parcel, on the slopes of the Rittersberg mountain, just below the ruins of the thirteenth century Ortenbourg castle, about a mile west of the village itself. There is no grand cru in the vicinity, but wines are labeled Rittersberg, which indicates granitic terroir. The top wines are labeled as Réserve Personnelle and come from vines more than 60-years old. Wines are fermented in stainless steel and aged in demi-muids.

Domaine Roland Schmitt

50 rue-des-Vosges, 67310
Bergbieten
+33 3 88 48 57 12
Julien Schmitt
cave@roland-schmitt.fr
www.roland-schmitt.fr

10.5 ha; 50,000 bottles [map p. 34]

Located in far north of the region, the Schmitt family has had vineyards in Bergbieten since the seventeenth century. Roland Schmitt started working in the vineyards when he was 14 and took over in 1982 in his twenties. After he was killed in an automobile accident in 1993, his wine Anne-Marie (Italian by origin) took over the domain, and now runs it with their two sons, Julien and Bruno. The style tends to be dry. The top wines come from Glintzberg and grand cru Altenberg de Bergbieten. The Rieslings are dry.

Domaine Maurice Schoech

4 route de Kientzheim, 68770 Ammerschwihr

+33 3 89 78 25 78

Jean-Léon & Sébastien Schoech

domaine.schoech@free.fr

www.domaineschoech.com

18 ha; 65,000 bottles
[map p. 36]

The Schoech family have been here since 1650, but moved into wine production when Maurice Schoech built his cellar in the village in 1973. Sons Jean-Léon and Sébastien are now at the domain. A third of the holdings are in grand crus Kaefferkopf, Mambourg, Schlossberg, and Furstentum, and unusually there is also a plot in Rangen at the far south of the appellation. From Kaefferkopf there are both Riesling and Gewürztraminer, as well as an unusual cuvée of 25% Riesling with 75% Gewürztraminer from a plot where the varieties are intermingled. Riesling and Pinot Gris also come from lieu-dit Sonnenberg, a south-facing granite-based slope, where the vineyard was assembled parcel by parcel.

Henri Schoenheitz

1 rue de Walbach, 68230 Wihr-au-Val

+33 3 89 71 03 96

Henri Schoenheitz

cave@vins-schoenheitz.fr

www.vins-schoenheitz.fr

16 ha; 85,000 bottles
[map p. 37]

A little off the beaten track, in the Vallée de Munster to the west of Colmar, the vineyards are on steep slopes that go up to elevations of 550m. The domain was founded in 1812, more or less destroyed during the second world war, and then replanted in the 1960s. Grapes were sold to the cooperative until Henri started estate bottling. In fact, Henri, helped by his son Adrien since 2014, is the sole vigneron in the commune who undertakes estate bottling. The top wines come from several lieu-dits, with Herrenreben perhaps the best. As Adrian describes the style, "We really want very pure, very mineral and elegant wine, so we use mainly steel tanks."

Domaine Christian Schwartz

8 Rue de l'Ungersberg, 67650 Blienschwiller

+33 3 88 92 63 06

Christian Schwartz

christian.schwartz67@free.fr

www.vins-christian-schwartz.fr

7 ha [map p. 35]

Christian has run this family domain since 1988. Vineyards are in Blienschwiller and the neighboring communes of Dambach-la-Ville and Epfig. The entry-level range has Edelzwicker, Pinot Blanc/Auxerrois, Pinot Gris, and Riesling. The Collection Marine comes from specific terroirs: Gewürztraminer from lieu-dit Haguendon, and Pinot Gris and Riesling from the granite of grand cru Winzenberg. There are two Pinot Noirs: Tradition ages in cuve, and the Vieilles Vignes comes from 40-year-old vines and ages in barriques. There is Gewürztraminer Vendange Tardive.

Domaine Albert Seltz

21 rue Principale, 67140 Mittelbergheim

+33 3 88 08 91 77

Albert Seltz

info@albert-seltz.fr

www.albert-seltz.fr

13 ha; 60,000 bottles [map p. 34]

This domain is unusual for its focus on Sylvaner. It was founded in 1557, and Albert took over from his father in 1980. Passionate about Sylvaner, he fought for the decision to allow it to be included in the grand cru Zotzenberg. He produces several cuvées of Sylvaner: Sylvaner De Mittelbergheim (varying from dry to off-dry depending on the vintage), Sylvaner Vieilles Vignes Sono Contento (late harvest, off-dry), Vieilles Vignes from Zotzenberg (usually off-dry), and a Vendange Tardive, La Colline Aux Poiriers. From Zotzenberg there are also Riesling and Gewürztraminer.

102

Fernand Seltz et Fils

42 rue Principale, 67140
Mittelbergheim
+33 3 88 08 93 92
Michel Seltz
seltz.michel@wanadoo.fr
www.facebook.com/domaineseltzfernand

10 ha; 40,000 bottles [map p. 34]

This family domain has been in the center of Mittelbergheim for several generations. The best wines come from grand cru Zotzenberg, including Riesling, Pinot Gris, Gewürztraminer, and Sylvaner (one of the reference points for the cru). Riesling from the calcareous lieu-dit of Brandluft is also notable.

Domaine Étienne Simonis

2 Rue des Moulins, 68770
Ammerschwihr
+33 3 89 47 30 79
Étienne Simonis
cave@vins-simonis.fr
www.vins-simonis.fr

7 ha; 40,000 bottles
[map p. 36]

The family has been growing grapes in Ammerschwihr since the seventeenth century. René Simonis took over in 1969 and built the winery in 1975. Étienne Simonis took over this small family domain from his father in 1996, and moved from selling off some of the crop to bottling all production. Vineyards include Grand Crus Kaefferkopf (planted with Riesling and Gewürztraminer on a mix of granitic and calcareous soils) and Marckrain (planted with Gewürztraminer). Another important terroir is lieu-dit Vogelgarten (in the valley between the Kientzheim and Sigolsheim, where the soil is clay and calcareous marl like Marckrain, but the exposure is cooler, giving less exuberant Gewürztraminer). Pinot Gris and Riesling are planted on the granitic terroir of Le Clos des Chats. More than a third of plantings are Gewürztraminer. Wines are aged in stainless steel or wood depending on the vintage.

Domaine Philippe Sohler

80 A Route du Vin, 67680
Nothalten
+33 3 88 92 49 89
Philippe Sohler
contact@sohler.fr
www.sohler.fr

11 ha
[map p. 35]

Philippe Sohler grew up making wine with his grandfather and uncle, and established the domain in 1997; his daughters Lydie and Marine joined him in 2016, moved the domain to organic, and focused on dry wines. The 60 separate vineyard parcels are around the village of Nothalten (south of Barr). The entry-level range, Les Origines, has all the varieties. The range Les Sol'Aires comes from specific lieu-dits: Clos Rebberg Pinot Gris is from schist while Zellberg (sweeter) is from calcareous terroir; Fronholz Gewürztraminer is from calcareous clay; Riesling comes from the sandstone-granitic terroir of Heissenberg and from the volcanic terroir of grand cru Muenchberg. There are also Vendanges Tardives from Pinot Gris and Gewürztraminer and SGN Gewürztraminer. Wines age in cuve, except for Clos Rebberg and the Matéo Pinot Noir, which age in barriques.

Domaine Sylvie Spielmann

2 Route de Thannenkirch, 68750 Bergheim
+33 3 89 73 35 95
Sylvie Spielmann
sylvie@sylviespielmann.com
www.sylviespielmann.com

8 ha; 55,000 bottles
[map p. 36]

The domain is located around an old gypsum quarry, so the soils are relatively heavy. (The family was producing gypsum until 1969.) Sylvie returned from winemaking in the New World to take over the property from her mother in 1988. The best wines come from grand cru Kanzlerberg (where the domain is one of only three producers in this tiny grand cru of 3 ha). In addition to the varietal wines, GypsE, sublabeled Terroir Unique, pays tribute to the family background by comprising a blend of Pinots (Blanc, Gris, and Noir) from a plot planted on the old quarry in 2004 with the varieties intermingled.

Domaine Vincent Stoeffler

1 Rue des Lièvres, 67140 Barr
+33 3 88 08 52 50
Vincent Stoeffler
info@vins-stoeffler.com
www.vins-stoeffler.com

16 ha; 120,000 bottles
[map p. 35]

Vincent's father founded the estate in the 1960s, and Vincent has been running the domain since 1986. The domain expanded after Vincent's marriage,. and now has vineyards from both sides of the family, with a group around Barr from Vincent's side, and a group around Riquewihr from his wife's side. The top wines come from Kirchberg de Barr and Schoenenbourg (just outside Riquewihr), and also the lieu-dits Kronenburg and Muhlforst. In addition to Riesling, there are Pinot Gris and Gewürztraminer from Kirchberg. The Riesling tends to be not quite dry, with around 6-7 g/l residual sugar.

Domaine Trapet Alsace

14 rue des Prés, 68340 Riquewihr
+33 3 80 34 30 40
Andrée & Pierre Trapet
message@trapet.fr
www.domaine-trapet.fr/alsace

15 ha; 35,000 bottles
[map p. 36]

After Andrée Grayer married Jean-Louis Trapet and moved to Gevrey Chambertin, she wanted to retain her connection with Alsace, and in 2002 took over the family vineyards, which became Domaine Trapet Alsace. Most of the vineyards are in Riquewihr or adjacent Beblenheim, with the largest holdings comprising about one and a half hectares each of Riesling and Gewürztraminer in the two villages. There are also five grand crus, headed by the most substantial holding, Schoenenbourg. In addition, Minima is a blend of 6 six varieties which is produced without any sulfur. Aging takes place either in the traditional wooden foudres, or, Trapet being a committed biodynamic producer, concrete eggs.

Domaine de la Vieille Forge

5, rue de Hoen, 68980 Beblenheim
+33 3 89 86 01 58
Denis Wurtz
domainevieilleforge68@orange.fr
www.domainedelavieilleforge.com

10 ha

The name of the domain which Denis Wurtz inherited from his grandparents, refers to the family background. It's located in a sixteenth century house in Beblenheim. Vineyards are broken up into many small parcels — Denis even calls them micro-parcels — in Bennwihr, Beblenheim, Zellenberg, Riquewihr, Ribeauvillé, and Kientzheim, including four grand crus, Sporen, Sonnenglanz, Mandelburg, and Schoenenbourg . Wines that stand out are the Riesling Silex, a selection from the bets terroirs, Pinot Noir, aged in barriques, Gewürztraminer from Sporen and Sonnenglanz, and Pinot Gris from Sonnenglanz, which usually is discernibly sweet (around 32 g/l residual sugar).

Domaine Wach

5 Rue Commanderie, 67140 Andlau
+33 3 88 08 93 20
Pierre Wach
info@guy-wach.fr
www.vins-wach.fr

8 ha; 45,000 bottles
[map p. 35]

The Wach family started as coopers in 1748 and later they became growers. Guy Wach created the domain in 1976, and his son Pierre (the seventh generation) took over in 2017. (The formal name of the domain is Domaine des Marroniers but now Guy Wach figures larger on the label.) A new cellar was completed in 2010. Vineyards include 1 ha in grand crus Kastelberg, Moenchberg, and Wiebelsberg. Wines age traditionally in foudres, including some that are 200 years old. There is a full range of all the varieties, with Riesling from each of the grand crus; Kastelberg is the largest production.

Domaine Jean Michel Welty

24 Grand Rue, 68500 Orschwihr
+33 3 89 76 09 03
Jean-Michel Welty
vinswelty@gmail.com
www.welty.fr

10 ha
[map p. 38]

Located at the foot of the Bollenberg hill, this family domain dates from 1738; Jean-Michel took over in 1984, and now has been joined by his son Jérémy. In addition to the entry-level range, there's a complete range of wines, Les Naturels, vinified without added sulfur. The top cuvées are the Pinot Gris, L'Or Gris, from Bollenberg, Gewürztraminer Aurélie (quite sweet with 45-55 g/l residual sugar), and Riesling from, grand cru Pfingstberg. From Pinot Noir, there are rosé, L'Ancestral (aged in cuve), and Quintessence (aged in barriques). There's also a range of Vendange Tardives and SGN, including Pinot Gris, Gewürztraminer, Riesling, and Muscat, as well as Crémant and eaux-de-vie.

Wolfberger

6, Grand-Rue, 68420 Eguisheim
+33 3 89 22 20 20
Joseph Erhrart
contact@wolfberger.com
www.wolfberger.com

1300 ha; 14,000,000 bottles
[map p. 37]

This is an important cooperative, representing about 10% of the Alsace vineyards, with a correspondingly large range of wines, with 300 cuvées altogether, including a large amount of Crémant. Founded in 1902, it represents 420 growers, with a concentration around Eguisheim where it has 200 ha. Vineyards include 50 ha in 15 grand crus. It has 6 boutiques extending the length of Alsace from Strasbourg to Guebwiller. When Domaine Lucien Albrecht collapsed in 2012, Wolfberger bought the brand and vineyards. Lucien Albrecht had been the second-largest exporter of Alsace wines to the United States, so this was a significant addition to the cooperative. Wolfberger also owns Maison Willm, a large negociant. The Albrecht and Willm names continue as brands of Wolfberger.

Zeyssolff

156 Route de Strasbourg, 67140
Gertwiller
+33 3 88 08 90 08
Céline Zeyssolff
info@zeyssolff.com
www.zeyssolff.com

10 ha; 100,000 bottles
[map p. 35]

Founded in 1778, since Yann Zeyssolff took over in 1997, the enterprise has expanded to include a "wine space", which has a delicatessen and a tea room. At the small wine-producing estate, production is expanded by a small negociant activity, buying grapes from about 6 ha from growers in the village). The estate has some holiday cottages. Wines include all seven varieties of Alsace, with Klevener de Heiligenstein (the rosé variant of Traminer) as a specialty, in this case slightly sweet with 29 g/l residual sugar. The top wines come from grand cru Zotzenberg, with Sylvaner, Muscat, Pinot Gris, Gewürztraminer, and Riesling. There are also Vendanges Tardive and SGN.

Ziegler-Mauler Fils

2 rue-des-Merles, 68630 Mittelwihr

+33 3 89 47 90 73

Philippe Ziegler

vins.zieglermauler@orange.fr

www.vins-ziegler-mauler.fr

4.5 ha; 35,000 bottles

[map p. 36]

Philippe Ziegler took over this small family domain from his father in 1996. Vineyards are around the villages of Mittelwihr, Ammerschwihr, and Kaysersberg, with the top holdings in grand crus Kaefferkopf and Schlossberg. The policy is minimal intervention, so sometimes fermentation does not complete, and the wines show residual sugar. The domain is known for its Gewürztraminer.

Domaine Zinck

18 rue des Trois-Châteaux, 68420 Eguisheim

+33 3 89 41 19 11

Philippe Zinck

info@zinck.fr

www.zinck.fr

20 ha; 160,000 bottles

[map p. 37]

From an old winemaking family, Paul Zinck established the domain in 1964 with 2 ha. His son Philippe is in charge today. The domain uses estate grapes for its three ranges: Portrait is the entry-level; Terroir comes from higher-altitude vineyards near Eguisheim; and there are four grand crus, Eichberg, Pfersigberg, Goldert, and Rangen. The Crémant comes from purchased grapes. The wines seem to be moving towards a drier style. The domain has a spacious tasting room.

Glossary of French Wine Terms

Classification

There are three levels of classification, but their names have changed:

- *AOP* (Appellation d'Origine Protégée, formerly AOC or Appellation d'Origine Contrôlée) is the highest level of classification. AOPs are tightly regulated for which grape varieties can be planted and for various aspects of viticulture and vinification.
- IGP (Indication Géographique Protegée, formerly Vin de Pays) covers broader areas with more flexibility for planting grape varieties, and few or no restrictions on viticulture and vinification.
- Vin de France (formerly Vin de Table) is the lowest level of classification and allows complete freedom with regards to varieties, viticulture, and vinification.
- INAO is the regulatory authority for AOP and IGP wines.

Producers

- Domaine on a label means the wine is produced only from estate grapes (the vineyards may be owned or rented).
- Maison on the label means that the producer is a negociant who has purchased grapes (or wine).
- Negociants may purchase grapes and make wine or may purchase wine in bulk for bottling themselves. Some negociants also own vineyards.
- Cooperatives buy the grapes from their members and make the wine to sell under their own label.

Growers

- There is no word for winemaker in French. The closest would be oenologue, meaning a specialist in vinification; larger estates (especially in Bordeaux) may have consulting oenologues.
- A vigneron is a wine grower, who both grows grapes and makes wine.
- A viticulteur grows grapes but does not make wine.
- A régisseur is the estate manager at a larger property, and may encompass anything from general management to taking charge of viticulture or (commonly) vinification.

Viticulture

- There are three types of viticulture where use of conventional treatments (herbicides, insecticides, fertilizers, etc.) is restricted:
- Bio is organic viticulture; certification is by AB France (Agriculture Biologique).
- Biodynamique is biodynamic viticulture, certified by Demeter.
- Lutte raisonnée means sustainable viticulture (using treatments only when necessary). There are various certifications including HVE (Haute Valeur Environmentale).

- Selection Massale means that cuttings are taken from the best grapevines in a vineyard and then grafted on to rootstocks in order to replant the vineyard.
- Clonal selection uses (commercially available) clones to replant a vineyard.
- Vendange Vert (green pruning) removes some berries during the season to reduce the yield.

Winemaking

- Vendange entière means that whole clusters of grapes are used for fermentation.
- Destemming means that the grapes are taken off the stems and individual berries are put into the fermentation vat.
- Fermentation (or Vinification) intégrale for black grapes is performed in a barrique, standing up open without an end piece. After fermentation, the end is inserted and the wine ages in the same barrique in which it was fermented.
- During fermentation of red wine, grape skins are pushed up to the surface to form a cap. There are three ways of dealing with it:
- Pigeage (Punch-down) means using a plunger to push the cap into the fermenting wine.
- Remontage (pump-over) means pumping up the fermenting wine from the bottom of the vat to spray over the cap.
- Délestage (rack-and-return) means running the juice completely out of the tank, and then pouring it over the cap (which has fallen to the bottom of the vat)
- Chaptalization is the addition of sugar before or during fermentation. The sugar is converted into alcohol, so the result is to strengthen the alcoholic level of the wine, not to sweeten it.
- A cuve is a large vat of neutral material—old wood, concrete, or stainless steel.
- Cuvaison is the period a wine spends in contact with the grape skins.
- Battonage describes stirring up the wine when it is aging (usually) in cask.
- Soutirage (racking) transfers the wine (without the lees) from one barrique to another.
- Élevage is the aging of wine after fermentation has been completed.
- Malo is an abbreviation for malolactic fermentation, performed after the alcoholic fermentation. It reduces acidity, and is almost always done with redwines, and often for non-aromatic white wines.
- A vin de garde is a wine intended for long aging.

Aging in oak

- A fût (de chêne) is an oak barrel of unspecified size.
- A barrique (in Bordeaux or elsewhere) has 225 liters or 228 liters (called a pièce in Burgundy).

- A tonneau is an old term for a 900 liter container, sometimes used colloquially for containers larger than barriques, most often 500 or 600 liter.
- A demi-muid is a 600 liter barrel.
- A foudre is a large oak cask, round or oval, from 20-100 hl.

Sweet wines

- Moelleux is medium-sweet wine.
- Liquoreux is fully sweet dessert wine.
- Doux is sweet (usually not botrytized) still or sparkling wine.
- Mutage is addition of alcohol to stop fermentation and produce sweet wine. The style is called Vin Doux Naturel (VDN).
- Passerillage leaves grapes on the vine for an extended period so that sugar concentration is increased by desiccation.
- Botrytis, also known as noble rot, means grapes have been infected with the fungus Botrytis cinerea, which concentrates the juice and causes other changes.

Index of Estates by Rating

Index of Organic and Biodynamic Estates

Index of Estates by Name